Sarah Flower, a**　　　　　**：ery books, is passionate about healthy ea**　　　　**sugar-free and low-carb way of eating. She has trained with *The Real Meal Revolution*'s Prof Noakes and Jonno Proudfoot.

Sarah writes for a number of publications including *The Daily Mail*, *Top Santé* and *Healthista*. She appears regularly on BBC Radio Devon and BBC Radio 4 *Woman's Hour*.

ALSO BY SARAH FLOWER

The Busy Mum's Plan-ahead Cookbook

Eat Well, Spend Less

The Healthy Lifestyle Diet Cookbook

The Healthy Halogen Cookbook

The Healthy Slow Cooker Cookbook

Perfect Baking with Your Halogen Oven

Halogen Cooking for Two

The Everyday Halogen Family Cookbook

The Everyday Halogen Oven Cookbook

Slow Cook, Fast Food

The Low-Carb Slow Cooker Cookbook

THE SUGAR-FREE FAMILY COOKBOOK

Sarah Flower

A *How To* Book

ROBINSON

ROBINSON

First published in Great Britain in 2017 by Robinson

Copyright © Sarah Flower, 2017

13 5 7 9 10 8 6 4 2

IMPORTANT NOTE
The recommendations in this book are solely intended as education
and information and should not be taken as medical advice.

A CIP catalogue record for this book
is available from the British Library.

ISBN: 978-1-47213-888-0

Typeset in New Caledonia by Hewer Text UK Ltd, Edinburgh
Printed and bound in Great Britain by CPI Group (UK) Ltd, Croydon CR0 4YY

Papers used by Robinson are from well-managed forests and other responsible sources.

Robinson
An imprint of
Little, Brown Book Group

nt of Little, Brown Book
ve first-hand experience
k, its target market and
@howtobooks.co.uk.

To my amazing Dad. You taught me to work hard and never give up on what I believe in. I blame you for my dogged determination to spread the healthy eating message. I hope I made you proud. I love you and miss you every day.

CONTENTS

FOREWORD

W E live in curious medical times. As science and technology advance, we are increasingly able to treat previously incurable diseases and provide previously unimagined palliative care. Yet, at the same time, we find ourselves in the throes of the most widely spread and expensive health catastrophe in history: the obesity epidemic.

While it may seem that many of the global population is facing health risks as a result of malnutrition, the sad truth of the modern world is that obesity and its related syndromes are causing even more damage to our collective health. In Britain, 62 per cent of adults are classed as overweight; of these, 28 per cent are obese.

I was born in 1984. Back then, famine and malnutrition were headline health issues, while diabetes, obesity and high blood pressure were rarely reported on. Today, however, the 'diseases of obesity' are seen as almost inevitable conditions for those approaching middle age. In my lifetime, global health has deteriorated, and it has become crystal clear that we have been getting something very wrong.

In 2013, I was fortunate to be part of a national health turnaround in South Africa following the launch of a book I co-authored. *The Real Meal Revolution* has sold over 275,000 copies to date and spawned a new understanding of and approach to eating, focusing on low-carbohydrate high-fat (LCHF) nutrition. We exposed politicians, farmers and scientists for creating the obesity epidemic – whether intentionally or not – by offering the wrong nutritional advice to the entire western world.

Since the 1970s global health guidelines have advised us to avoid fat and encouraged us to eat carbs (directly) and sugar (indirectly). In creating a cookbook that spurned this advice in favour of eating fat and avoiding carbs, we have witnessed first-hand how people have simultaneously solved their weight problems and reversed their health problems. The effects have been so dramatic that some readers have reported curing themselves of Type 2 diabetes, which was previously believed to be an incurable disease.

The reason our book has sold so many copies (and has been published internationally) is because our advice works. Removing sugar and refined carbs from the diet is now considered by most doctors in South Africa as the key treatment for Type 2 diabetes and obesity management, as it should be around the world.

Sarah Flower is one of the many inspiring nutritionists I've encountered on my journey of nutrition and health discovery in recent years, a bright-smiling dietary soldier in the battle for better health. Sarah's book is filled to the brim with everything you need to remove sugar and refined carbs from your diet. Critically, her recipes will make this lifestyle change feel less restrictive and more indulgent – exactly what you need to make it sustainable.

What we eat has a profound effect on our health and our lifestyles. Food is indeed our medicine and eating real food that is free from processed junk is the way to improve your health and your life. Sugar-free, home-cooked food is the future of healthcare and, if you ask me, Sarah's treatment – in the form of Southern Fried Chicken, Rhubarb Crumble and Chocolate Pecan Meringue Cake – is just what the doctor ordered.

Jonno Proudfoot
The Real Meal Revolution
www.realmealrevolution.com

INTRODUCTION

SUGAR and refined carbohydrates are now seen to be the root cause of many of our western diseases as well as our obesity crisis. Since the low-fat revolution started in the 1970s, we have been increasing our reliance on carbohydrates and sugars. Our bodies are simply not designed for the excessive consumption of carbohydrates. Diabetes, fatty liver disease, heart disease, arthritis, Alzheimer's, obesity, metabolic syndrome . . . the list goes on and on.

I started reducing sugar several years ago but didn't go completely sugar-free until 2014. My youngest son has Asperger's syndrome and I have seen a dramatic improvement in his behaviour when he is not eating sugar. It is not easy to ensure your child is 100 per cent sugar-free, especially if they are a teenager, but doing your best in the home really does make a massive difference to their health.

The last few years have seen a massive increase in awareness of the dangers of sugar. It has been an exciting time for nutritionists such as myself, expanding on the benefits of increasing natural fats as well as working on new ways to ensure we can satisfy our sweet cravings without adding sugar.

This book is a go-to guide of family recipes and pantry essentials to help you and your family on your sugar-free journey. Most recipes also adhere or can be adapted to be very low carbohydrate and grain free. This helps those who are struggling to cut the cravings when going sugar-free.

I hope you enjoy the book. You can also follow my work at www. sarahflower.co.uk and join my Facebook group Everyday Sugarfree. Best of luck with your sugar-free journey.

Sarah x

1

SUGAR AND ITS EFFECT ON OUR HEALTH

We all need to cut our sugar consumption. In 2015, the World Health Organisation (WHO) set new guidelines. It recommended adults and children reduce their daily intake of free sugars to less than 10 per cent of their total energy intake. A further reduction to below 5 per cent or roughly 25 grams (6 teaspoons) per day would provide additional health benefits. Pour 6 teaspoons of sugar into a glass and you can see it is quite a substantial amount, but, shockingly, some low fat yoghurt desserts can contain more than the maximum set per day. Looking at the amount of sugar in our food, is it easy to see why we are on average consuming 30–40 teaspoons per day.

Free sugars refer to monosaccharides (such as glucose and fructose) and disaccharides (such as sucrose or table sugar) added to foods and drinks by the manufacturer, cook or consumer, and sugars naturally present in honey, syrups, fruit juices and fruit juice concentrates.

'We have solid evidence that keeping intake of free sugars to less than 10 per cent of total energy intake reduces the risk of overweight, obesity and tooth decay,' says Dr Francesco Branca, Director of WHO's Department of Nutrition for Health and Development. 'Making policy changes to support this will be key if countries are to live up to their commitments to reduce the burden of noncommunicable diseases.'

The WHO guidelines do not refer to the sugars in fresh whole fruits and vegetables, and sugars naturally present in milk, because there is no reported evidence of adverse effects of consuming these sugars.

Since the low-fat revolution in the 1970s, we have been consuming more and more carbohydrates, especially refined carbohydrates and sugars. We are seeing an epidemic of children and adults suffering from diabetes, obesity, heart disease and a host of related problems.

But do we really understand sugar? Let's get down to basics.

- Sugar is made up of 50 per cent glucose and 50 per cent fructose but has no nutrient value and it is not needed by the body. You could live quite happily without any added sugar.

- There are many names for sugar – maple syrup, honey, molasses, agave syrup, high fructose corn syrup, barley malt, cane sugar, sucrose, maltose, maltodextrin, ethyl maltol, lactose and the list goes on. These all affect the body in the same way.

- Carbohydrates (think flour, pasta, bread, sugar, vegetables, beans, grains and starchy foods such as potatoes) get converted into glucose, providing us with energy. However, we are consuming more than we have ever eaten in our existence and it is this excess consumption that is so detrimental to our health. Our bodies can run extremely well on fat, protein and low carbohydrates. There are numerous studies showing the benefits to health when limiting sugar and carbohydrates, particularly in reversing diabetes and heart disease.

- Fructose is now deemed by many to be the most damaging form of sugar. Fructose is naturally present in fruit. Eating a whole fruit means you are also eating some fibre, which slows down the digestion of the fructose. However, fruit juice does not contain fibre, therefore a high concentration of fructose floods the liver. Your fresh orange juice in the morning contains more sugar than a glass of cola. Studies have also shown that when you drink pure fructose, it turns off your leptin response, meaning you don't get the signal to tell you when you are full.

How sugar affects our health

Glucose in our bloodstream is harmful so our pancreas secretes a hormone called insulin which basically transports the glucose to be stored as glycogen in our liver or muscles. However, with our western diet, our natural stores in our liver and muscles are full to capacity, which means our bodies push the glucose into our cells to be stored as fat. When you calculate the amount of sugar and carbohydrates we are consuming daily, you can see why we are getting fatter and fatter.

Insulin also puts a hold on us burning fat reserves so once we are fat, we will stay fat – particularly fat around the middle – until we limit our sugar and carbohydrate consumption. High insulin levels not only mean a larger waistline, but very serious implications for our overall health.

There is a very long list of health complaints that experts believe stem from sugar. It is a very scary list and, if you are like me, it will be enough to focus the mind and dig deep to maintain a sugar-free lifestyle.

This is not a definitive list, but just really the tip of the iceberg.

Obesity	Heart disease
Diabetes	Depression
Metabolic syndrome	Hyperactivity
Alzheimer's	Anxiety
Arthritis	Insomnia
Auto immune disease	Inflammation
Fatty liver disease	Inability to concentrate

High blood pressure	Appendicitis
High cholesterol	Haemorrhoids
Low immune system	Varicose veins
Cancer	Osteoporosis
Tooth decay	Food intolerances
Learning difficulties	Gout
Candida	PMS
Thrush	PCOS
Gallstones	Mood swings

The truth about fructose

This is the real baddie and is incredibly damaging. Fructose is metabolised in the liver. The liver doesn't know how to deal with high levels of fructose as there is no real requirement for it in the body. There are many health implications from a high-fructose diet.

- Non-alcoholic fatty liver disease, caused by fat (triglycerides) being stored in the liver, is increasing – especially in children – and can lead to cirrhosis of the liver.

- Any remaining triglycerides get pushed out into our bloodstream to cause a whole range of health issues, including heart disease and cellular damage, particularly to the arterial walls.

- Fructose increases uric acid production, which can lead to high blood pressure, gout and kidney stones.

- High fructose can increase waistlines and increased adipose tissue (fat) around vital organs. We are now seeing TOFI (thin outside fat inside) youngsters, who look thin but their internal organs have excess fat surrounding them, which can be incredibly damaging.

- Your bowel health can be affected. Bad bacteria feed off the sugars in your diet, particularly fructose. Poor bowel health not only affects your digestion and bowel habits but also lowers your immune system and can increase your risk of tumours. Poor bowel health also impacts how your body deals with cholesterol.

- Leptin is a hormone that tells your brain when you are full. Fructose effectively turns off your leptin response, making it very easy for you to overeat.

- Ghrelin is a hormone that tells us when we need to eat. Fructose and insulin mess with this hormone, stimulating it to make its presence heard, encouraging us to eat more and more. Lack of sleep can also affect this hormone which is why shift workers find it harder to lose weight.

- Fructose can increase whole body inflammation and can increase your risk of oxidative damage in your cells. It also has a detrimental effect on your looks as it interferes with your collagen production – your skin loses elasticity and your risk of wrinkles is increased.

What do we need to avoid?

Avoiding added sugar and foods high in fructose is an absolute must. You will find sugar in a variety of guises on food labels, so be vigilant. You also need to be aware of the free sugars – these are the naturally occurring ones and those added to the food in a supposedly natural state. Think of fruit juices, syrups, honeys. It is a minefield but the simple thing is to read the labels and to try as much as possible to make your own food from scratch.

You also need to be aware of the foods that convert to glucose once consumed. The carbohydrates and starches not only add to your daily sugar load but also spike insulin and increase food cravings, so to be successful when going sugar-free, you really need to watch your carbohydrate intake, particularly from refined carbohydrates. Net carbs are carbohydrates with the fibre taken out (as fibre does not get absorbed so those following a low-carb diet go on the net carbs).

Read the label

Labelling is not as straightforward as it should be with the food manufacturers apparently trying to confuse us. You need a calculator to work out serving sizes per gram and then convert that into teaspoons in order to get a better idea of how much you are consuming. When you read the amounts per teaspoon it is very scary.

Here are some names you need to avoid:

Sucrose, Fructose, High Fructose Corn Syrup, Barley Malt, Dextrose, Maltose, Agave Nectar, Beet Sugar, Cane Juice, Turbinado Sugar, Caramel, Carob Syrup, Corn Syrup, Date Sugar, Dextrin, Evaporated Cane Juice, Fruit Juice, Grape Juice, Diastase, Glucose, Maltol, Palm Sugar, Monoglycerides, Refiners Syrup, Mannose, Oligofructose, Tapioca Syrup, Maple Syrup, Treacle, Saccharose, Molasses, Coconut Sugar, Polydextrose, Glycerine, Yakon, Dextran, Diastatic Malt Powder, Sorghum, Ethyl Maltol, Galactose, Golden Syrup, Honey, Inverted Sugar, Lactose, Maltodextrin, Muscovado Sugar, Oat Syrup, Avena Sativa, Panela, Panocha, Crystalline Fructose

Artificial sweeteners

I avoid artificial sweeteners as I have read too many papers linking their use to mental health problems and health complaints. There is mounting evidence to show that artificial sweeteners are highly addictive, increase your sugar cravings and continue to lead to obesity. Many of my clients were addicted to sugar-free/diet fizzy drinks. They are one of the first things we have to remove from their diet in order to move to better health and weight loss.

Natural sweeteners

There is a lot of misinformation regarding sugar-free. Some people choose to be free of refined sugar, instead opting for maple syrup, agave or honey. However, a word of warning. You are still taking in sugars in the form of glucose and, most worryingly, fructose. Your body metabolises sugars in the same way whether they are from refined or natural sources, so really, you are just taking a sideways step. You will also continue to crave sweet foods so it will make your sugar-free journey so much harder.

One of the main objectives of this book is to help you train your palate off sugar and sweet cravings; so you don't want to swap one sugar for another alternative. By all means use the natural sweeteners as a transition towards becoming sugar-free, but gradually reduce all types of sweeteners as your palate changes. I hardly use any natural sweeteners in my food now as I find them sweet enough.

Recommended sweeteners

The three sugar alternatives I would recommend – stevia, xylitol and erythritol – are fructose free, meaning they have very little adverse impact on my health.

Although my recipes include these sweeteners, I must emphasise that the key is to use these as treats to help you in the transition phase of becoming sugar-free and not to overdo the sweet hits.

Stevia is a wild plant from the subtropical forest in North East Paraguay. The leaves of stevia contain glycosides of which sweetening power is between 250 and 400 times their equivalent in sugar. Stevia contains no calories and no carbohydrates. It does not raise blood sugar or stimulate an insulin response, so for many, it is the preferred choice.

Stevia is very very sweet and the cheapest of all three, but it does have a strange aftertaste which is hard to control. I have found liquid stevia has less aftertaste but it is really trial and error and depends on the brand you use. I have also found some people are more sensitive to the aftertaste than others. Plus, you need very tiny amounts so using it can be a bit of a juggling act to start with.

Stevia is very hard to gauge in recipes as it is very much down to personal taste, product and the person's sensitivity to the aftertaste. If you are new to this you may prefer to use xylitol or erythritol, but if you are a fan of stevia, you can still follow my recipes, but add stevia to suit your own personal taste.

Xylitol (sold as Total Sweet in supermarkets) looks just like sugar. Xylitol may sound slightly odd, but the word is derived from the Greek word for wood, 'xyl', as in xylophone, because the natural sugar alternative was first discovered in birch wood. Xylitol has now been found in a host of other plants and fruits, such as sweetcorn and plums, but is still largely extracted from birch and beech wood in Europe today.

Xylitol looks and tastes just like normal granulated sugar, but it has a host of benefits. It has 40 per cent fewer calories than normal sugar and less than 50 per cent of the available carbohydrates (those that are utilised by your body), but it does contain carbohydrates and therefore does stimulate an insulin response so is not suitable for everyone.

Xylitol can have a laxative effect in some people and if eaten to excess: this is because xylitol attracts water. This effect is different from one person to the next and can change as your body gets used to xylitol. The lower your body weight the less xylitol it takes to cause the effect, so children can be affected more. As a general rule daily consumption should be limited to 5g–10g per 10kg of body weight (adults and children alike).

You also need to keep xylitol, or any food made with it, well clear of dogs. As with grapes and chocolate, dogs metabolise xylitol quite differently to humans and it can be very dangerous for them even in small amounts. Don't be tempted to give your dog anything with xylitol in, no matter how small.

The UK's leading brand of xylitol is Total Sweet (www.totalsweet. co.uk). Made from sustainable European birch and beech wood, it is available in most supermarkets.

Erythritol (found in blends from companies such as Natvia and Sukrin) is, like xylitol, a sugar alcohol. You can buy this as icing sugar, white sugar and brown sugar. Use this as a direct replacement in recipes, but be aware that manufacturers often add stevia to these blends as erythritol on its own is not so sweet, so you may still detect a slight aftertaste.

Unlike other low-calorie sugar substitutes, erythritol contains zero calories. Erythritol does not affect blood sugar or insulin levels during or after consumption, making it safe for diabetics and for those following a low carb high fat (LCHF) diet.

Unlike other sugar alcohols, such as xylitol, maltitol and isomalt, erythritol is well absorbed from the digestive tract, passed into the urine and eliminated from the body, so does not have a laxative side effect.

Fruit

Eat whole fruits and avoid fruit juices or concentrates. I tend to opt for berries which are lower in fructose. Fill up with nutritious vegetables but don't binge on whole fruits. If you like juices or smoothies, opt mainly for vegetable-based drinks with only a very small amount of added fruit. This way you will gain the essential nutrients and antioxidants but limit your consumption of damaging fructose.

Fat

I know this chapter is all about sugar but we can't discuss avoiding sugar without talking about increasing our natural fats. I know there is a huge resistance to eating fat; we have been conditioned for so long to believe that fat is bad for our health, it is hard to overcome this, but please, believe me when I say, you need to eat plenty of good healthy fats!

We have shunned fat since the low-fat revolution but we need fats for optimum health. Aim to get these from natural sources such as oily fish (a great source of omega 3), seeds, flax oil, coconut oil, olive oil and nuts. Avocados are a great source of healthy fat. I advise butter instead of the heavily processed margarines. Eat the fat from grass-fed meat. This is all food in its natural state. Avoid processed fats such as trans-fats and fried foods. I only use coconut oil, olive oil and butter in cooking, with olive oil or flax oil on my salads.

Fats do not make you fat! Our bodies need healthy fats; they are vital for almost every function in our body – hormones, skin, brain, joints, etc. High insulin caused by a diet of refined carbohydrates and sugars causes weight gain and a whole host of other ills. A low fat diet is really a high carbohydrate diet. A diet rich in carbohydrates and sugars also increases your food cravings, whereas a diet rich in natural, healthy fats keeps you full and satisfied.

I avoid all margarines, spreads and oils apart from a very good quality olive oil, flax oil, butter and coconut oil.

My recipes include full fat milk, cream, full fat cheese, eggs, nuts and seeds, coconut oil and butter. This is accompanied by fresh vegetables, oily fish and good quality meat. The message is to eat real food and avoid processed food, sugar and refined carbohydrates.

2

KEEPING OUR CHILDREN HEALTHY

As any mum, I have been increasingly concerned about the health of our children. I am passionate about educating children and parents about real food and I teach cookery and healthy eating in schools across the country.

I often have rather heated debates about the honesty, or rather lack of, of the food industry and the blatant tricks they play, particularly on our children. Some of the foods targeted towards children are the unhealthiest in the supermarket. The food industry targets the young, as once they have their loyalty, they have them for life. They spend billions of pounds formulating their products to achieve 'The Bliss Point' who enough sugar to be addictive but not enough to be sickly sweet. We are surrounded by temptation to eat more and more processed, sugary food. We are being conditioned from birth to have ever sweeter, chemically-induced, palates and suffer from peer pressure, emotional pulls, and less and less healthy options, even in our hospitals and schools.

We need food industry regulation, especially for foods aimed at our children, and we need to regulate our advertising policies, preventing misleading health messages and food labelling, particularly to our children.

Weaning your baby

If you are planning to have children or have recently had a baby, you are at the right stage to introduce a sugar-free lifestyle. It is far easier to wean a child into this way of life, rather than try to change a child's palate and habits once established. You really need to feed your child fresh, real food, cooked at home. Mash your own vegetables, feed your child what you are eating, just purée and freeze to save time. Encourage your child to be less reliant on sugars and carbohydrates.

Bring baby into the kitchen when you are cooking. Pop them into a high chair and let them watch you cook. Give them some safe toys such as a wooden spoon to bash or some plastic bowls to play with. As they get older you can get them to help you or copy what you are doing. A bit of mixing, tasting, feeling and even throwing on the floor is a good way of engaging with food.

A quick scan of my local supermarket revealed some packaging that can really tempt the new mum. There is an abundance of baby products that claim to be natural foods – but they're not! Pouches of fruit purées, vegetables and then you get to the snack foods – animal-shaped biscuits, lots of corn snacks – as well as a mass of ready meals.

The World Health Organisation make the following recommendations – read this and then compare it to what we are seeing on our supermarket shelves. Remember, the WHO recommends less than 5 per cent of the daily expenditure to be from sugar AND free sugars (meaning naturally occurring sugars, fruit concentrates etc.).

'For infants and young children

In the first two years of a child's life, optimal nutrition fosters healthy growth and improves cognitive development. It also reduces the risk of becoming overweight or obese and developing non-communicable diseases later in life.

A word about fruits

A lot of the products aimed at your baby and toddler contain fruits and fruit concentrates. You really are better off giving your child whole fruits. Even though the whole fruit contains sugar in the form of fructose, the sugar is encased in fibre so your child won't digest the whole amount of fructose, plus your child will feel full when eating whole fruit, whereas when fruit is used as a sweetener or in juices and snacks these will turn off the feeling of fullness. It is also a good idea to limit the amount of sweet foods you are feeding your baby and toddler as you don't want to encourage a sweet palate.

As your child grows

If you have weaned your child on a sugar-free diet, keeping him or her sugar free should be a breeze, but for those of us who are trying to reverse our families' reliance on sugar and processed foods, this can be a much trickier process.

Get the children in the kitchen to experiment with cooking food, and to explore new tastes and textures. They will enjoy creating new recipes and buying the ingredients to make healthy meals.

Educate. Children are incredibly receptive to knowledge but it has to be introduced gently. Don't lecture them, but encourage them to talk about food. Just like adults, children need to know why something is bad for them in order to dampen any cravings.

Encourage alternatives. It is no good simply stating the child can have no sugar ever again. You need to show them that you can be sugar-free but not miss out on any of the foods they love. Get them into the kitchen to bake and create using sugar-free sweeteners until their palate changes. You may find in the first few months you make far more sweet stuff as you prove it is not a restrictive diet. As your palate changes, you will need the sweet foods less and less.

The teen years

The teenage years are a really difficult time to keep your child in line with a healthy diet. You don't want to go into battle with a moody, hormonal teenager but you also need to ensure they are getting a good diet, especially to help balance those raging hormones!

> You have to give children the freedom to make some of their own food choices but this has to be coupled with good food education. It is harder to control as they become more independent and all you can do is provide good foundations and hope that they will naturally revert to the healthier choices.

The right tools. It is important as your child is facing adulthood to give them the tools to make the right decisions in life. Get them in the kitchen to prepare their own meals and snacks. Ensure they have good, nutrient-dense ingredients to hand and show them how to make food from scratch rather than rely on processed foods. Congratulate them on their accomplishments and encourage them to experiment. We will always need to feed ourselves, so cookery is a vital skill.

Taking control. As they grow, teenagers will be less inclined to sit and eat as a family, choosing instead to take more control of their mealtimes and food. Make things nice and easy by preparing a range of healthy, homemade ready meals to keep in the freezer, enabling them to eat in a hurry if they need to.

Image is everything. Teenagers are often prone to peer pressure so you don't want to alienate them too much. For some, knowledge and being a bit different is a good thing, so embrace that; for others, there is nothing worse than a nagging mum who wants you to eat weird food when all they want to do is eat the same as everyone else. If the latter is your child, then try to make food that appeals – low carb pizza, healthy southern fried chicken, etc. You will find all the recipes in this book.

Feed the body not the hormones. If you can, try to feed nutrient-dense foods to help balance those raging hormones and encourage good nourishment. Teenagers are growing into adults and require plenty of good nutritious food. It may seem like they eat everything in sight, but keep focused and provide the right foods and snacks. My eldest son was as skinny as a rake but ate almost continually. It was exhausting trying to keep up with his insatiable appetite.

• Skin problems can be helped by avoiding processed sugary food. High glycaemic foods stimulate insulin which increases sebum production in the skin, so opt for low GI foods. Sugar also upsets the bacterial balance of your skin, bowel and mucus membranes, making it more prone to outbreaks and infection. Dairy products can also exacerbate acne. If your hormonal teen is reluctant to change, give them some literature or, even better, some links to YouTube lectures on how sugar can affect the skin. Look at their diet and add plenty of antioxidant-rich foods, and encourage them to drink plenty of water to help flush the system. Zinc and vitamin C can also dramatically help with acne. If you are unsure of the nutrient value of their food, you may want to add a supplement – a good multivitamin with extra magnesium is a good starting point. Many girls are prescribed the contraceptive pill to help with acne; this is something I would strongly advise you avoid.

- Ensure girls have plenty of iron and magnesium in their diet to help them through the early stages of menstruation. Iron-rich foods include meat, seafood, beans and green leafy vegetables – but remember you also need to have adequate vitamin C in order to absorb the iron. If in doubt, add a good quality supplement. Opt for magnesium and iron in citrate form as this is the most useable, bioavailable source.

- Plenty of sleep is vital not just for balancing their moods but also to help keep their weight stable and avoid carb-loading days due to lack of sleep. It may seem like your teen sleeps all morning but not at night, which can be frustrating – the only good thing is they are not acting all sullen, moody and only offering grunted replies when they are sleeping!

Energy drinks – Avoid, Avoid, Avoid. This is where you really need to be the big boss and help to keep them off these horrendous drinks. There is a huge amount of research and scary videos on the internet to help strengthen your case against these awful drinks. They are not good at any age and you can really help your teenager by firmly discouraging them from developing a fizzy drink addiction. The combination of high caffeine and large amounts of sugar can cause extreme moods, elevated heart rate, depression, insomnia and hyperactivity, to name but a few!

General rules for all ages

There are some general rules to adopt for all families. These really do help when you are breaking free from sugar and processed foods.

Treats don't have to be food. We have to be very careful when we start offering food treats to our children. Apart from the health implications this has to do with social and emotional conditioning. I work with clients whose whole association with food is embroiled around their emotions. They were given treats/comfort food when they were happy, sad, celebrating, consoling, lonely, bored and partying. It all starts with treats for our children. A toddler falls over so you rush to console with a sweet. Go to see Grandma and get some sweets as a treat. Been good at school, let's go and buy a burger. The list goes on and on. Break these rules and start to use non-food as treats. Done well at school – a new game or trip to the cinema. Falls over, a cuddle and a comforting story from their favourite story book. Ask Grandma to put the sweets away and invest in a game, magazine or colouring book instead.

No sugar at home. It sounds simple, but keeping your home sugar-free is a massive help when you are changing to this way of eating. It is so difficult when one person in the family refuses to eat the same as everyone else. Go through your cupboards and swap the everyday foods for sugar-free alternatives. You cannot control what goes on outside your home, but you can control what is happening inside. It is easier to avoid temptation when it is not staring you in the face.

Plan ahead – really important at all times but especially when you have children. Ensuring you have sugar-free snacks to hand will keep your children happy and keep you focused on your goal. Breakfasts can be difficult for busy homes. Breakfast cereal was always the nice and easy option but many breakfast cereals are really just bowls of sugar. Plan ahead. Look at the breakfast chapter in this book for lots of ideas.

3

CREATING HEALTHY CELEBRATIONS

MANY parents are concerned when it comes to birthdays and celebrations. We don't want to be seen to be cruel to our children by not giving them the same as their peers, but in providing 'treat' foods we are not thinking about how these can affect our health. We can, however, do a lot to create a healthy celebration which is still enjoyable, fun and appealing for the children.

Birthday parties

Children's birthday parties often mean a massive amount of quick, easy, processed food, but you can provide a wonderful healthy spread without too much effort. You need to consider age groups and also check if any of the guests have allergies – particularly nuts, as we tend to use these a lot in our food.

Fun and games

Plan your activities and prizes so that the focus is not on food. You don't have to spend a fortune to offer gifts, goody bags or prizes that are not food related. The rise in pound shops means we have an abundance of little prizes for very little outlay. Young children can have toys and older children can have make-up, stationery or gadget accessories.

Party food

If you are going to a party venue that includes food, try to opt for the healthiest food and speak to the venue in advance about swaps that can keep your food as sugar-free as possible. You may have to be a bit more creative when it comes to drink options – sparkling water with some natural flavourings is a good choice. There is a new brand on the market called Ugly, which offers cans of sugar-free, sweetener-free sparkling drinks. I am a huge fan. Remember to think about things like ketchup, mayonnaise and dressings – you may need to provide your own.

Savoury ideas

- **Vegetable crudités with some dips** (see *The Pantry* chapter for dip recipes) – kids love these, especially younger children.

- **Pizza** – I am talking homemade, of course! You can make this with a traditional base, or a low-carb or grain-free alternative (see *Fast Food* chapter).

- **Burgers** – homemade burgers are super-easy and very filling (see *Healthy BBQ* chapter). Remember, you will need to make your own sugar-free sauces (see *The Pantry* chapter).

- **Sausages in blankets/cocktail sausages on sticks** – wrap sausages in bacon or simply place cocktail sausages onto cocktail sticks.

- **Cheese** is great to nibble on. Add some to cocktail sticks or slice into strips or chunks for children to add to their plate.

- **Eggs** – make egg mayonnaise or serve hard-boiled eggs, cut in half or stuffed with your favourite filling, or make your favourite frittatas.

- **Mini quiches** – these are like little gems, packed with protein. You can include vegetables, but if you have fussy children, cheese, onion and bacon might be best. Look at other savoury dishes such as sausage rolls in the *Savoury Snacks & Lunches* chapter too.

- **Cheese straws/biscuits** – invest in some cookie cutters and you can make these in a variety of shapes to suit the theme of the party.

- **Potato wedges** – always a hit, especially for older children. Top with a variety of herbs and spices.

- **Crisps** – swap potato crisps for some spiced nuts (make sure your party guests are able to eat nuts), Parmesan crisps or kale crisps. See *The Tuck Shop* chapter.

Sweet ideas

You will find a lot of suitable recipes in *The Bakery* chapter, but you can also adapt your favourite cake recipes by swapping the sugar for a sugar alternative such as xylitol.

- Homemade ice-cream is always a hit. Combine it with some sugar-free jelly (see the chapters on *The Ice-cream Parlour* and *Just Desserts*).

- Have a look at *The Tuck Shop* chapter for some homemade sugar-free sweets and treats the kids will love, such as Faux Ferrero Rocher (really too good for children!), jelly bears, chocolate bark and coconut ice.

Birthday cake

When it comes to the all-important birthday cake, you can use your favourite cake recipe and replace the sugar for your natural sweetener. Xylitol and erythritol blends can be used as a direct replacement for sugar, though I personally would still reduce the amount. You can also use the erythritol blended icing mixes, which are good, or see *The Bakery* chapter for other cake icing ideas – my favourite is the chocolate ganache.

Christmas

The average Brit consumes over 6,000 calories on Christmas Day, but there are ways to lighten the load and still enjoy the festivities:

- You are less likely to make bad food choices if you plan in advance. Plan your meals, and fill your freezer with homemade ready meals to eat when you are busy.
- Before you go out to party, ensure you have eaten a good healthy meal. You are less likely to over-consume and it will help line your stomach if you do over-indulge a little on the bubbly!

Cakes and sweet treats

Technically you can only make Christmas cake and Christmas puddings free from refined sugar as they are packed with dried fruit, which is very high in natural sugars. If this suits your lifestyle, simply follow your favourite recipes and eliminate the added sugar. Beware these are naturally high in sugar, so not advisable if you are starting out on sugar-free.

If you want a lighter pudding, opt for a cheesecake, a pavlova, fruit salad, homemade ice-cream, chocolate mousse or panna cotta – all found in the *Just Desserts* chapter.

For a chocolate Yule log, see my chocolate roulade recipe in *The Bakery* chapter, as topped with chocolate ganache it makes a wonderful Yule log.

For chocolates and nibbles, take a look at *The Tuck Shop* chapter for inspiration, including chocolate mint bites, Faux Ferrero Rocher, fudge, coconut ice and jelly bears. You will also find ideas for crisps and flavoured nuts. Try dipping satsuma segments in dark chocolate for a tasty spin on a chocolate orange.

Halloween

Halloween is getting more and more commercial, so you may want to explore sugar-free options for parties or for trick or treat food. Check out *The Tuck Shop* chapter for confectionery options. If you are having a party, there are many party foods you can use, but also have some fun and get creative.

Ghoulish party food ideas

- Homemade creamy pumpkin soup – you can even serve this in carved out mini pumpkins for a real statement.
- Peeled whole clementines make wonderful mini pumpkins, with a stick of celery as a pumpkin stalk.
- Cheese straws made into finger shapes, with almond slithers as fingernails.
- Devilled eggs, topped with a spider – make the body with half a black olive and cut the remaining half into tiny slithers for legs.
- Ghost bananas, cut in half, with some currants or dark chocolate chips to make the eyes and mouth.

- Apple dentures, carve out the teeth and lips in apple quarters.

- Homemade sugar-free cupcakes, topped with a variety of spooky toppings – colour your frosting orange, to make pumpkin cupcakes.

- Make some ghoulish looking sugar-free jelly – so easy!

- Buy Halloween silicon moulds to make your own jellied sweets, gummy worms or chocolates – look at the cake decorating sections of stores or online.

4

THE BREAKFAST TABLE

OVER the last fifty years or so we have completely transformed our breakfast habits. What used to be a meal of eggs, kippers, bacon or kedgeree is now one of sweetened cereal, sugar-packed juice, toast and jams. Is it any wonder we are all suffering from sugar overload? It is estimated that most children consume 10–15 teaspoons of sugar before they leave for school in the morning.

So what can you feed your family in the mornings? I understand that most parents are time-stretched and maybe that pack of sugary cereal is the lifesaver when you are in a hurry, but with a little bit of weekly preparation, you can make breakfast quick, healthy and nutritious.

Eggs are an amazing complete food: they not only fill you up but also provide some fantastic nutrients. It only takes minutes to rustle up a scrambled egg and this is far more nutritious than sugary cereal. You can also make mini frittata muffins, which can be frozen and heated in the morning, or made the day or evening before, or consider hard-boiled eggs.

Avocados are packed with healthy fats and are really filling. Mash a ripe avocado and serve on toast on its own or mix with hard-boiled eggs for a yummy egg/avo mayonnaise. Serve avocado slices with your bacon and egg.

Porridge is very healthy, served with some berries, chopped nuts and seeds, but also look at the lower-carb option of chia porridge – it is packed with protein and can be mixed with a variety of flavours.

Pancake mixture can be made up the night before, or if you are really short of time, cook the pancakes beforehand and heat gently in the microwave before serving with some berries and a dollop of yoghurt.

A savoury breakfast can be filling and nutritious. There is nothing in the rule book to state you have to have a sweet breakfast. Try bacon and eggs, salmon, or my spinach, bacon and egg one pot.

AVOCADO, POACHED EGG & BACON OPEN TOASTIE

One of my absolute favourite starts to the day.

Serves 2

6 rashers of back bacon
2 eggs
2 slices of rye bread or grain-free bread
1 avocado, mashed
seasoning to taste

- Cook the bacon in a sauté pan or under the grill.
- Boil water in the kettle, ready to poach the eggs.
- Fill a saucepan with the boiling water and poach the eggs, either directly in the water, or in poach pods (in which case pop on a lid and leave to simmer for 5 minutes).
- Toast the bread.
- Spread the mashed avocado onto the toast. Add your poached eggs and season with salt and black pepper before topping with bacon. Serve immediately.

44g fat, 30g net carbohydrates, 5.4g fibre, 40g protein per serving

For a lower carb option omit the rye bread, which brings the carbohydrates down to 1.2g per serving, with 2.4g of fibre.

MINI FRITTATA MUFFINS

So easy and great for a breakfast or packed lunch. You can prep these the night before, ready to pop into the oven in the morning. I add whatever vegetables need using up in my fridge – peppers, spring onions, courgettes, tomatoes or spinach. You can also use leftover cooked vegetables. For purposes of the nutritional analysis, I used 60g of spinach and 60g of red onion.

Makes 6

4 eggs, beaten
1 tbsp butter, melted
100ml milk
1 tsp dried oregano or mixed herbs (optional)
seasoning to taste
6 tbsp vegetables of your choice, finely chopped
60g cheese of your choice, grated or crumbled

- Preheat the oven to 190°C/gas mark 5.
- Place the eggs in a jug with the butter, milk, herbs and seasoning. Beat well until combined.
- Grease your muffin tray.
- Divide the finely chopped vegetables and grated cheese among six sections of the muffin tray.
- Pour in the egg mixture until the muffin cups are two thirds full.
- Pop into the oven and bake for 20 minutes until golden. They will rise but will drop again as they cool. Don't worry, they still taste divine!

9.7g fat, 1.7g net carbohydrates, 0.6g fibre, 8.3g protein per muffin

SPINACH, BACON & EGG ONE POT

A really nourishing yet simple way to start the day. You can use kale instead of spinach if you prefer but it won't wilt like spinach does.

Serves 2

1 tsp coconut oil or butter
6 rashers of bacon
60g baby leaf spinach
4 eggs
50g feta cheese, crumbled
Seasoning to taste

- Place a sauté pan on a medium heat, add the coconut oil or butter.
- Add the bacon and fry gently for a few minutes on each side. Make sure the bacon covers the base of the pan.
- Add the baby leaf spinach over the bacon. Crack the eggs onto the spinach. Finish with the crumbled feta. Season to taste.
- Pop the lid onto the pan and leave to cook for 5–8 minutes until the eggs are cooked.
- Serve immediately.

44g fat, 0.8g net carbohydrates, 1.2g fibre, 45g protein per serving

CHOCO-NUTTY GRANOLA

Really easy to make, there is nothing stopping you doubling or tripling the recipe to make up a large batch as it keeps well in a sealed, airtight container.

Makes approx. 15 servings

300g mixed nuts (brazil, hazelnuts, almonds, macadamia, walnuts)
100g pecan nuts (these add a sweetness kids love)
75g flaked almonds
100g coconut flakes
75g sunflower seeds
75g pumpkin seeds
150g oats
50g coconut oil
2 tbsp cocoa or cacao powder
2 tbsp xylitol or erythritol blend (or to taste)

- Preheat the oven to 150°C/gas mark 2.
- Place the nuts in a freezer bag and bash with a rolling pin until they are in smaller pieces. I prefer doing this because a food processor tends to over-process them and if you are not careful you can end up with nutty dust!
- Place the crushed nuts in a bowl with the coconut flakes, seeds and oats.
- Melt the coconut oil in a jug, then add the cocoa and sweetener and combine well.
- Pour over the nut/seed mix and stir well until the oil coats all the nuts.
- Pour the mixture onto a large baking tray – you may need two trays, depending on their size. Spread until it covers the tray.

- Pop into the oven and bake for 5 minutes before turning the nuts and baking for another 5 minutes.

- Remove from the oven and cool before storing in an airtight container.

32g fat, 11.1g net carbohydrates, 5.8g fibre, 9g protein per serving

For low carb/grain free, omit the oats. Carbohydrates 4.7g, fibre 5g per serving.

AVOCADO BOATS

Avocados are packed with nutrients: add an egg and you have a real powerhouse of a breakfast. I love these, you can prepare them the night before if you prefer, but really they take minutes to prepare and 15 minutes to cook. You can also have these for lunch.

Serves 2

1 avocado
3 rashers of cooked bacon or 3 slices of ham, chopped (optional)
2 eggs
40g grated cheese
seasoning to taste

- Preheat the oven to 180°C/gas mark 4.
- Cut the avocado in half and remove the stone. You may want to scoop out some of the flesh to make a larger hole.
- Add a little chopped bacon or ham to each avocado half.
- Place the avocados on a baking tray. Crack the eggs and place one in each avocado half.
- Finish with a sprinkle of grated cheese and season to taste.
- Pop into the oven and bake for 10–15 minutes until the eggs are cooked.

38g fat, 1.3g net carbohydrates, 2.4g fibre, 7g protein per serving

BASIC CHIA PORRIDGE

Chia seeds are packed full of protein, so I use them a lot in cooking. They absorb liquid so they're a great thickener, which is why I use them in my sugar-free jams. This recipe is for a basic chia porridge – you can add more flavours, using fruit (such as a mashed banana), a spoonful of cacao powder or cocoa, or shredded coconut. Top with nuts or berries. The porridge needs to be prepared at least an hour in advance, but ideally the night before.

Serves 2

4 tbsp (60g) chia seeds
150ml full fat milk (use coconut or almond milk if you prefer)
1 tsp sugar-free vanilla extract (optional)
sprinkle of sweetener to taste (I use Sukrin Gold)

- Place the chia seeds and milk in a bowl or jug. Stir in the vanilla extract.
- Leave to rest in the fridge for an hour or overnight.
- You can eat this hot or cold. I prefer hot so I gently warm in a pan until it is heated through, adding more milk if needed.
- Finish with a sprinkle of sweetener and some nuts and berries.

12.1g fat, 5.6g net carbohydrates, 11.6g fibre, 8g protein per serving

CINNAMON NUT GRANOLA

Granola is really easy to make and there is nothing stopping you doubling or tripling the recipe to make up a large batch as it keeps well in a sealed, airtight container. Don't add any fruit to the granola until after you have baked it as it has a tendency to burn. Personally I would only add some goji berries, if anything, as you need to remember that dried fruit really is nature's candy.

Makes approx. 15 servings

300g mixed nuts (brazil, hazelnuts, almonds, macadamia, walnuts)
100g pecan nuts
60g flaked almonds
100g coconut flakes
75g sunflower seeds
75g pumpkin seeds
50g flaxseeds
200g oats
50g coconut oil
2 tsp ground cinnamon
2 tbsp xylitol or erythritol blend (or to taste)
75g goji berries (optional)

- Preheat the oven to 150°C/gas mark 2.
- Place the nuts in a freezer bag and bash with a rolling pin until they are in smaller pieces.
- Place the crushed nuts in a bowl with the coconut flakes, seeds and oats.
- Melt the coconut oil in a jug, then add the cinnamon and sweetener and combine well.

- Pour over the nut/seed mix and stir well until the oil coats all the nuts.

- Pour the mixture onto a large baking tray and spread until the tray is covered.

- Pop into the oven and bake for 5 minutes before turning the nuts and baking for another 5 minutes.

- Remove from the oven and cool. Add your goji berries before storing in an airtight container.

33g fat, 16.1g net carbohydrates, 6.9g fibre, 10.2g protein per serving

For low carb/grain free, omit the oats and the goji berries. Carbohydrates 4.3g, fibre 5.5g per serving.

PANCETTA, SPINACH & RICOTTA FRITTATA

This is one of my absolute favourite starts to the day. This is more of a brunch or a weekend treat. It is really tasty hot or cold.

Serves 4

2 tsp butter
200g diced pancetta or lardons
1 small red onion, finely diced
4 eggs
250ml single cream
seasoning to taste
2 handfuls (60g) of baby leaf spinach
150g ricotta

- Place the butter in a large sauté pan.
- Add the pancetta and onion and cook on a medium heat.
- While that is cooking, place the eggs in a jug, add the cream and season to taste with black pepper and a pinch of salt. Beat well until combined.
- When the pancetta has started to crisp up, reduce the heat to low and pour in the egg mixture. While it is still wet, add the spinach leaves and push into the top of the egg mix.
- Preheat the grill.
- Dollop the ricotta around the pan. Leave on the low heat for 2 minutes before transferring to your grill.
- Grill until golden and bubbling on the top and until it is firm.
- Serve immediately.

53g fat, 4g net carbohydrates, 0.7g fibre, 32g protein per serving

BUTTERMILK PANCAKES

You can make the batter in advance and store it in the fridge until you are ready to fry the pancakes. Serve with berries and Greek yoghurt for a sweet-tasting, but still sugar-free, start to the day.

Makes 8 small pancakes

3 eggs
150ml buttermilk
150g plain flour or almond-flour
½ tsp baking powder
1 tsp butter

- Place the eggs in a large jug and beat well. Add the buttermilk and continue to whisk.
- Beat in the flour and baking powder, whisking to remove all lumps.
- When ready to fry, add a little butter to your sauté pan. Once melted, add dollops of batter.
- Once the base has started to colour, you can flip the pancakes and cook until both sides are lovely and golden. Pop on a plate and fry the next batch, adding more butter if needed.
- Serve with some berries and Greek yoghurt.

3.2g fat, 14.7g net carbohydrates, 0.7g fibre, 5g protein per pancake

For low carb/grain free, use almond flour instead of plain flour. Carbohydrates 2.2g, fibre 2.4g.

SWEET BERRY FRITTATA

I've popped this into the breakfast chapter, but I also enjoy it for a quick supper if I don't have much of an appetite. I love it served with cream or Greek yoghurt. I don't bother with sweetener, but if you are new to sugar-free, you may want to add some xylitol, erythritol or a touch of stevia to taste.

Serves 2

3 eggs
150ml single cream or full fat milk
1–2 tsp xylitol or erythritol (optional)
butter or coconut oil
handful of berries (raspberries and blueberries are best)

- Preheat the grill.
- Beat the eggs, cream or milk and sweetener together in a jug.
- Heat a sauté pan on a medium heat. Add a little butter or coconut oil to prevent sticking.
- Pour the egg mixture into the pan, tipping the pan from side to side to spread the liquid. Leave to cook for 1–2 minutes before adding the berries. I drop these in randomly.
- Cook for another minute before removing from the heat.
- Pop under the grill for 5 minutes or until it is puffed up and golden.
- Serve hot or cold with Greek yoghurt or double cream.

22g fat, 3.2g net carbohydrates, 2.3g fibre, 13.6g protein per serving

5

SAVOURY SNACKS, LIGHT LUNCHES & PACKED LUNCHES

So what is the best thing to have for lunch? It is quite simple, **Eat Real Food.** We all make so many excuses – too busy, real food is more expensive, can't cook, lack of education. We have lost the skills to make food from scratch and become more and more reliant on quick meal fixes that are, due to the manufacturing processes, often devoid of nutrients and full of sugar. Why do we have added sugar in our spice mixes, our ketchup, our mayonnaise, our pasta sauce, our baked beans? Almost 80 per cent of supermarket food contains sugar is it any wonder we are consuming so much of it?

Make your food at home using natural ingredients. You will not only save yourself from overconsumption of sugars, but you could also save a lot of money.

Ideas for packed lunches

Packed lunches can be mind-numbingly dull. On the other hand, they can be healthy and tasty, but it takes a little more time and effort. Rushing to fill your lunchbox with 5 minutes to spare before you dash out the door is not a good way to create a healthy sugar-free lunch. The secret, as always, is to plan ahead.

Use foods that are healthy and naturally sugar-free as the basis for your packed lunch.

- **Eggs** – hard boiled, as egg mayonnaise, scotch eggs, mini frittatas or quiche.

- **Nuts** – these are far healthier than crisps. See *The Tuck Shop* chapter for healthy crisp and flavoured nut recipes. Some schools have a no nut policy so check before you add these to your children's lunches.

- **Cheese** – you can buy individually wrapped cheese portions which are perfect for quick snacks and very filling.

- **Veg sticks** – these are great to munch on, especially with a little pot of dip.

- **Meats** – use up your meat leftovers. Roast chicken can make a great sandwich or a Caesar salad. I have also eaten the chicken fajita and chicken Southern fried in this book cold with a salad. Kids really love these. I also bake bacon in the oven (it goes nice and crisp) and then store it in an airtight container in the fridge. Great to add to sandwiches or chopped in a salad. Kids love cold mini sausages, but check the ingredients as they can contain lots of sugars and grains.

- **Tuna** – a bit smelly but tuna is very nutritious. I make up tuna mayonnaise and place in little pots to have with a salad.

- **Bread** – if you are making sandwiches, opt for the healthiest, most nutrient-dense bread possible and check for added sugars. Look for wholemeal bread with grains and seeds. Alternatively opt for a rye or spelt bread. For low carb/grain free, there are lots of low-carb bread recipes on the internet although these vary in success. I have had many a purple loaf due to psyllium husk issues! I prefer my grain-free crackers – great with dips and toppings. See recipe in this chapter.

- **Pizza** – check out the recipes in the *Fast Food* chapter as these are great cold in packed lunches.

- **Salads** – fill your container with salad but don't add the salad dressing until you are just about to eat or you will end up with a soggy mess by lunchtime.

- **Leftovers** – if you have access to a kitchen at work, why not take in your own food? Spend a day batch cooking, make individual portions and pop into the freezer. Get into the habit of making slightly more than you need when you cook your meals, and pop the leftovers into the freezer ready for another meal or lunch.

- **Treats** – see *The Bakery* chapter for ideas.

- **Yoghurts** – buy full fat natural Greek yoghurt. Add your own fruit, nuts or seeds to suit.

MEDITERRANEAN-STYLE TORTILLA

This is an ideal dish for using up any leftover vegetables – anything goes so experiment!

Serves 4

5 eggs
1 bunch of spring onions, finely chopped
1 red pepper, diced or thinly sliced
150g pancetta, diced
4 sun-dried tomatoes, chopped
50g Parmesan, grated
small handful of fresh herbs (basil, oregano or thyme, finely
    chopped)
seasoning to taste

- Preheat the oven to 200°C/gas mark 6.
- In a large bowl, beat the eggs, then add the remaining ingredients and combine.
- Thoroughly line a 20cm flan dish with greaseproof paper before pouring in the mixture.
- Cook for 20–25 minutes, until firm.
- Serve hot or cold with salad.

27g fat, 3.7g net carbohydrates, 1.7g fibre, 22g protein per serving

SPINACH & FETA FILO PIE

Serve this with a selection of fresh salads and new potatoes – perfect for a summer's evening. See ovenleaf for a grain-free option.

Serves 6

40g butter
1 pack (200g) of filo pastry
400g baby leaf spinach, roughly torn
300g feta cheese, crumbled
2 eggs, beaten
finely grated nutmeg to taste
seasoning to taste
50g mature cheddar, grated (optional)
sesame seeds, to sprinkle

- Preheat the oven to 200°C/gas mark 6.

- Melt the butter in a saucepan or microwave, making sure it does not burn.

- Brushing each sheet lightly with melted butter, layer 4–5 sheets of filo pastry in the base of a large pie dish, allowing the sheets to hang over the edge.

- Place the spinach in a colander and rinse with hot water until the spinach starts to wilt. Place this in a mixing bowl. Add the feta, beaten eggs and nutmeg, season well with black pepper and mix. If you like a cheesy dish, you can also add grated mature cheddar. Place the mixture into the pastry base.

- Bring the pastry edges up over the filling. Brush with melted butter. Scrunch up more filo sheets and place these in the centre, brushing with butter.

- Finish with a sprinkle of sesame seeds.
- Place in the oven and bake for 25–30 minutes, until golden and crisp.
- Serve hot or cold.

19.9g fat, 25g net carbohydrates, 2.4g fibre, 15.6g protein per serving

For a lovely low carb/grain free version, make a crustless pie and simply fill the dish without the filo pastry. 1g carbohydrate, 0.9g fibre per serving.

TOFU & SPINACH QUICHE

This quiche is one of my favourites and it is a big hit with meat eaters as well as vegetarians – most don't realise they are eating tofu! It can be adapted for grain-free (see overleaf for ingredient substitutions if needed). It is also very simple to make and there's no risk of a soggy, eggy middle that some quiche recipes can suffer from!

Serves 8

175g spelt, buckwheat or wholemeal flour
75g chilled butter, cut into small pieces
400g tofu
1 bag of baby leaf spinach (approx. 80–100g)
75g mature cheddar, grated
1 red onion, finely chopped
dash of finely grated nutmeg
seasoning to taste

- To make the pastry, place the flour in a large bowl and add the chilled butter. Using your fingertips, rub the butter into the flour until the whole mix resembles breadcrumbs. Add 5–6 tablespoons of cold water (a little at a time) and mix until it forms a dough. Wrap the dough in cling film and place in the fridge to rest until needed.

- Preheat the oven to 200°C/gas mark 6. Grease a 23cm flan tin.

- Roll out the pastry on a floured surface and use to line the flan tin. Place a sheet of baking parchment over the pastry and cover with baking beans.

- Bake for 10 minutes. Remove the baking beans and parchment and cook for a further 10 minutes until the pastry starts to colour. Remove the pastry case from the oven and turn the oven down to 180°C/gas mark 4.

- Meanwhile, mash the tofu thoroughly. Place the spinach in a colander and rinse with hot water until it starts to wilt. Stir into the tofu. Add the grated cheese, onion and nutmeg. If the mixture is too dry, add a dash of milk and mix well. Season well before pouring into the pastry case.

- Bake in the oven for 20 minutes until golden.

- Serve hot or cold.

14.1g fat, 16.5g net carbohydrates, 2.9g fibre, 9.6g protein per serving

For low carb, opt for a crustless quiche, or for low-carb/grain-free pastry, rub 40g butter into 300g ground almonds and 75g ground hazelnuts. Add 2 eggs and seasoning to taste. Roll out between two sheets of baking parchment before lining your tin, then blind bake. 5.6g carbohydrates, 6.2g fibre per serving.

GREEN SQUEAK PATTIES

A great way to get some extra veg into your diet and to use up any left-overs you may have in your fridge. You can use cauliflower, broccoli, greens or even courgette for these little beauties. I like to cook them until golden and crispy.

Makes 10

1 head of cauliflower or broccoli, cut into florets
6 slices of bacon or pancetta, finely chopped
1 tsp butter or coconut oil
half bunch of spring onions, finely chopped
100g mature cheddar, grated
1 egg, beaten
1 tsp wholegrain mustard
seasoning to taste

- Steam your cauliflower or broccoli until soft.
- While it is steaming, fry the bacon or pancetta in a little butter or coconut oil until nice and crisp.
- Place the cauliflower or broccoli in a bowl and mash, or use a food processor.
- Once mashed, add the spring onions, cheese, crisp bacon/pancetta, egg and mustard and combine together thoroughly. Season to taste.
- Form into small patties; don't worry if they are lumpy as this is part of their charm.
- You can bake these patties or fry on both sides until golden. I bake for 20 minutes at 180°C/gas mark 4.

7.6g fat, 1.2g net carbohydrates, 0.6g fibre, 7.4g protein per patty

SAUSAGE ROLLS

You really need to buy good quality sausage meat. Check with your butcher or, if buying from a supermarket, read the label, as some sausage meat can contain an abundance of cereal fillers and even sugar.

Makes 12 sausage rolls

400g spelt, buckwheat or wholemeal flour
100g chilled butter, cut into small pieces
100g lard (or use a total of 200g of butter if you don't want to add
    lard), cut into small pieces
500g good quality sausage meat
1 small onion, finely chopped
2 tsp mixed herbs
1 egg, beaten
2 tbsp sesame seeds

- Preheat the oven to 190°C/gas mark 5.

- Place the Flour, butter and lard in a bowl.

- Using your fingertips, rub the fat into the flour until it resembles breadcrumbs.

- Add 5–6 tablespoons of very cold water and mix with a knife for a minute or so. Once a dough starts to form, use your hands to gently form into a ball. Don't handle it too much as pastry likes to stay cool.

- Wrap the dough in cling film and place in the fridge to rest for 20 minutes.

- In a bowl, mix the sausage meat, chopped onion and herbs together.

- Roll into 12 sausage shapes and leave to one side.

- Sprinkle flour onto a clean surface and roll out the pastry to form a rectangle.

- Place the sausage meat onto the centre of the pastry. Brush the top and bottom edges of the pastry with the beaten egg. Roll the pastry over the top of the sausages and push the pastry edges together firmly to form a good seal.

- Brush with beaten egg and sprinkle with sesame seeds. Cut into size before placing onto a baking tray.

- Bake for 25 minutes until golden.

26g fat, 23g net carbohydrates, 4g fibre, 11.7g protein per sausage roll

For low carb/grain free, see my Low-Carb Sausage Rolls recipe on page 57.

CRUSTLESS COURGETTE & SPRING ONION QUICHE

This is my mum's favourite; she makes a large dish and then has the slices cold with a salad for a quick and easy lunch. You can use any vegetables in this: it's a good recipe to use up the contents of your vegetable drawer. It is also nice with lumps of feta as well as the cheddar cheese.

Serves 8

2 courgettes, sliced
1 bunch of spring onions, finely chopped
50g baby leaf spinach
120g mature cheddar, grated
6 eggs, beaten
150ml full fat milk or single cream
1 tsp dried oregano
1 tsp dried parsley
seasoning to taste

- Preheat the oven to 190°C /gas mark 5.
- Place the courgette slices in a large ovenproof dish. Top with the remaining vegetables and cheese.
- Mix the eggs and milk or cream together in a jug until well combined. Add the herbs and season.
- Pour into the ovenproof dish to cover the vegetables.
- Place in the oven and cook for 30–40 minutes until it has risen and has a nice golden top.
- Eat hot or cold.

9.9g fat, 1.7g net carbohydrates, 1.1g fibre, 10.7g protein per serving

GRAIN-FREE LOW-CARB CRACKERS

This is more or less the same mixture as the flower's fat head pizza recipe in the *Fast Food* chapter and demonstrates how good the basic fat head dough can be. The secret to these is to make them as crisp as possible without burning them. Times are approximate as much depends on the efficiency of your oven and the thickness of your dough.

Makes 12 crackers

125g mature cheddar or mozzarella, grated
75g cream cheese
1 egg
100g ground almonds
½ tsp chilli powder
1 tsp dried oregano
seasoning to taste
1 egg, beaten (optional)
grated Parmesan to sprinkle (optional)

- Preheat the oven to 190°C/gas mark 5.

- Place the cheese and cream cheese in a bowl and pop into the microwave for 1 minute to soften (this makes it easier to form into a dough).

- Remove from the microwave and add the egg, almonds, chilli powder, oregano and seasoning, combining well. This will form a wet dough. Form into a ball.

- Put a large sheet of baking parchment on the worktop, and place the ball of dough in the centre. Put another sheet of parchment on top of the dough and press down with your hands (this is the easiest way to work the dough without getting sticky hands and worktop).

- Press into a rectangle or square shape using your hands and knuckles. The dough needs to be about ½cm thick.

- Place the whole thing, including parchment, onto a baking tray before removing the top sheet.

- Using a knife, gently score out your crackers. This makes it easier to cut them into perfect squares or rectangles once cooked. If you like, brush with beaten egg and sprinkle with Parmesan.

- Pop into the oven and cook until golden on top – this takes approximately 10 minutes.

- Remove from the oven and flip over, removing the bottom sheet of baking parchment. This helps to get the base of the crackers as crispy as the top.

- Pop back into the oven and cook until golden – approximately another 8–10 minutes. You can add more eggwash and Parmesan, if you wish.

- Remove from the oven and leave to cool on a cooling rack before breaking/cutting into crackers.

10.2g fat, 0.8g net carbohydrates, 1.1g fibre, 5.4g protein per cracker

CHEESE SCONES

Based on my favourite buttermilk scone recipe, these are really tasty. See overleaf for a low carb grain-free option.

Makes 6 scones

100ml buttermilk
1 egg, beaten
250g spelt, buckwheat or wholemeal self-raising flour
1 tsp baking powder
75g chilled butter, cut into small pieces
100g mature cheddar, grated, plus a little extra to sprinkle on the
    tops
½ tsp mustard powder
pinch of cayenne pepper or chilli powder
milk or beaten egg to brush the tops

- Preheat the oven to 200°C/gas mark 6.
- Combine the buttermilk and egg and leave to one side.
- Place the flour and baking powder in a bowl. Using your fingertips, rub the butter into the flour until it resembles breadcrumbs.
- Add the cheese, mustard powder, cayenne or chilli powder and combine well.
- Pour on the buttermilk mixture and stir with a wooden spoon. Once it starts to form a dough, you can use your hands to bring the dough together.
- Place onto a lightly floured board and press down to around 5cm thick
- Using a cutter, cut out six scones.

- Brush with milk or beaten egg and top with a sprinkle of cheese before placing in the oven.

- Cook for 12–15 minutes until golden.

Bacon, Cheese & Onion Scones – add 75g chopped cooked bacon and 1 cooked chopped red onion along with the cheese, which gives a fabulous flavour and something a little different from the standard cheese scone.

8g fat, 28g net carbohydrates, 4.5g fibre, 12.3g protein per scone

For low carb/grain free, swap the flour for 60g coconut flour and 190g almond flour or ground almonds. 5.5g carbohydrates, 7.8g fibre per scone.

LOW-CARB SAUSAGE ROLLS

These use a grain-free pastry – a basic recipe that is so versatile. I use a similar recipe as a base for pizza and also for grain-free crackers. It is a bit sticky to handle so arm yourself with some baking parchment. Be careful when buying your sausage meat as it often contains sugar and grains. Check the ingredients or speak to your butcher. You can also buy sausages and use these instead of the sausage meat if you prefer.

Makes 8 sausage rolls

250g cheddar or mozzarella, grated
120g ground almonds
1 tsp paprika
½ tsp chilli powder
1 egg, beaten
seasoning to taste
400g good quality sausage meat
1 tsp thyme
1 tsp sage
1 tsp parsley
1 egg, beaten, or milk, to brush the tops
2 tbsp sesame seeds

- Preheat the oven to 180°C/gas mark 4.

- Place the cheese in a bowl and pop into the microwave for 30–45 seconds to melt slightly.

- Add the ground almonds, paprika and chilli powder. Add the beaten egg and season well. Combine until it forms a dough. Leave to rest in the fridge for 10 minutes as this helps to firm it up.

- You may find this difficult to roll, so what I do is place the dough on a large sheet of baking parchment. I then top this with another large sheet of baking parchment and use my rolling pin or hands to flatten until it forms a rectangle and is roughly 1cm thick.

- In a bowl, mix your sausage meat with the thyme, sage and parsley. Season well.

- Shape your sausage meat into one long sausage or several smaller sausages (whatever is easier to handle) and pop these onto your dough – leaving enough pastry to comfortably roll over the top of the sausage.

- Brush the pastry with a little beaten egg or milk before wrapping the pastry over the top of the sausage, pressing down firmly. Cut into sausage rolls.

- Brush again with egg or milk and sprinkle with sesame seeds.

- Bake for 20 minutes until golden.

33g fat, 2.5g net carbohydrates, 2.6g fibre, 20g protein per sausage roll

GOATS CHEESE, PESTO & CHERRY TOMATO TART

This is a really simple quiche but it always looks impressive. Experiment with different wholegrain flours to create a lovely nutty flavour. See over-leaf for a grain-free option.

Serves 8

200g spelt, buckwheat or wholemeal flour
100g chilled butter, cut into small pieces
200g crème fraîche
3 eggs, beaten
3–4 tsp homemade sugar-free pesto (see *The Pantry* chapter)
seasoning to taste
125g goats cheese, cubed or crumbled
150g cherry tomatoes

- Preheat the oven to 200°C/gas mark 6. Grease a 23cm flan tin.

- To make the pastry, place the flour in a large bowl and add the chilled butter. Using your fingertips, rub the butter into the flour until the whole mix resembles breadcrumbs. Add 5–6 tablespoons of cold water (a little at a time) and mix until it forms a dough. Wrap the dough in cling film and place in the fridge to rest until needed.

- Roll out the pastry on a lightly floured surface and line your flan tin. Place a sheet of baking parchment over the pastry and cover with baking beans.

- Place in the oven and cook for 10 minutes. Remove the baking beans and parchment and cook for a further 10 minutes until the pastry starts to colour. Turn the oven down to 180°C/gas mark 4.

- Meanwhile, mix the crème fraîche, beaten eggs, pesto and seasoning together thoroughly and leave to one side.

- Place the goats cheese and cherry tomatoes in the pastry base. Pour over the crème fraîche mix.
- Bake for 30–40 minutes until golden.

28g fat, 17.6g net carbohydrates, 2.9g fibre, 11g protein per serving

For a low carb option, make a crustless quiche, or if you want a low carb/grain free pastry, rub 40g butter into 300g ground almonds and 75g ground hazelnuts. Add 2 eggs and seasoning to taste. Roll out between two sheets of baking parchment before lining your tin then blind bake. 4.5g carbohydrates, 5.7g fibre.

SCOTCH EGGS

I love these and think it's worth the time it takes to make them. Be careful when choosing your sausage meat as some can contain sugars and grains. Buy the best quality you can as it will make a huge difference.

Serves 4

5 eggs
400g good quality sausage meat
1 tsp thyme
1 tsp parsley
1 tsp sage
seasoning to taste
200g polenta (see grain-free option overleaf)
2 tsp paprika
oil for frying

- Boil the kettle. Place 4 eggs in a saucepan, pour over the boiling water and place on a medium heat. Boil for 8 minutes.

- Once cooked, immediately drain the hot water and run the eggs under cold water, before leaving in the saucepan filled with cold water.

- While the eggs are cooling, place your sausage meat in a bowl, add the thyme, parsley and sage and season well with salt and black pepper.

- Peel the eggs, discarding the shells.

- Divide the sausage meat into four pieces and form each piece into a ball. Flatten each ball as much as you can. Place an egg in the centre and wrap the sausage meat around the egg firmly until it is completely covered.

- In a bowl, add the remaining egg and beat well. Place the polenta and the paprika in another bowl, season and mix well.

- Dip each of the scotch eggs into the beaten egg before coating in the polenta mixture.

- Place on a sheet of greaseproof paper until you are ready to fry.

- Pour 5–6cm of oil into a pan or use your deep fat fryer. Heat the oil until hot (about 3–5 minutes), and then add your scotch eggs, turning until the whole egg is golden and crisp.

- Remove from the pan and drain on some kitchen paper.

- When cool, store in an airtight container.

NB: You can oven cook at 190°C/Gas mark 6 for 30 minutes, turning halfway through the bake.

29g fat, 38g net carbohydrates, 4.4g fibre, 27g protein per serving

For low carb/grain free, coat your scotch egg with ground almonds, coconut flour or even crushed pork scratchings. If you love bacon, you could wrap the outer edge with strips of it. Be aware of the contents of your sausage mix as it could contain grains. Using almond flour will give 6g carbohydrates, 7.2g fibre.

6

THE SOUP KITCHEN

SOUPS are incredibly nutritious and so easy to make, especially if you have a slow cooker. Be careful with shop-bought soups and read the label, as many can be full of sugar, salt and other nasties.

Soups are a great way of getting extra vegetables into your family. They are also cheap to make and very filling. Best of all, your favourite recipes won't need much adapting when following a sugar-free/low-carb diet. The main thing to be aware of is your stock.

Stock cubes and powder. At the time of writing, the only stock cubes I could find that were free from sugar are made by Kallo. They produce powders and cubes – but not all are sugar-free so you have to read the ingredients list. I like the beef bouillon powder (but the beef bouillon cubes contain sugar). You can also buy Marigold Swiss Vegetable Bouillon powder and Vecon concentrated vegetable stock. Most of these are available from health food shops but please check the label before buying.

Try to make your own stock as it is packed with nutrients, particularly if you use animal bones. You can freeze this stock so make in batches. See *The Pantry* chapter for recipes.

If any of the recipes below opt for stock and you don't want to make your own, you can add a teaspoon of yeast extract (check the label, Marmite is sugar-free but not all brands are) or Bovril (sugar-free, but not cubes) with warm water.

THAI-STYLE CHILLI, PRAWN & NOODLE SOUP

If you are hungry, this is a great quick and easy filler with protein-rich prawns, metabolism-boosting chilli and energy-giving noodles. You can use fresh or frozen prawns and whatever noodles you wish.

This recipe uses fish sauce and red Thai paste so please check the ingredients as they can contain sugar. See *The Pantry* chapter for my red Thai paste recipe. You can omit the fish sauce if you prefer.

Serves
1 tsp coconut oil
1 bunch of spring onions, finely chopped
2 cloves of garlic, crushed
1 red chilli, finely chopped
½ tsp chilli flakes
3–5cm piece of fresh ginger, finely chopped
200g tiger prawns, shelled and deveined
150ml coconut cream
400ml fish stock (sugar-free)
4 tsp fish sauce (sugar-free)
2 tbsp red Thai paste (see *The Pantry* Chapter)
150g rice noodles
handful of fresh coriander
seasoning to taste

- Place the coconut oil, spring onions, garlic, chillies and ginger in a sauté pan and cook for 3–4 minutes.

- Add the prepared prawns along with the coconut, fish stock, fish sauce and red Thai paste. Bring to a gentle simmer and cook for 5 minutes.

- Add the noodles and fresh coriander and cook for another 5 minutes before serving.

16.6g fat, 14.2g net carbohydrates, 2.7g fibre, 14.5g protein per serving

For low carb, omit the rice noodles. 5.9g carbohydrates, 2.2g fibre.

SQUASH SOUP WITH SPICED YOGHURT

This is nice in the autumn when squash is so readily available. I like the chilli yoghurt but if serving for children you can omit the chilli.

Serves 4

1 red onion, diced
1–2 cloves of garlic, crushed
1 tsp coriander seeds
butter or coconut oil for frying
1 butternut squash, diced
1 tsp ground coriander
2 tsp curry powder
1 cooking apple, diced
400–500ml vegetable stock or water
seasoning to taste
200g Greek yoghurt
1 red chilli (medium strength), finely chopped
1 tsp hot paprika

- In a large saucepan, sauté the onion, garlic and coriander seeds in butter or coconut oil for 3–4 minutes until beginning to soften.

- Add the butternut squash, ground coriander and curry powder and cook for a further 3–4 minutes.

- Add the apple before adding the stock or water. Put a lid on and cook on low-medium heat for 30 minutes until the vegetables are tender.

- Season to taste before liquidising.

- In a separate bowl, mix the yoghurt, chilli and paprika together.

- To serve, pour the soup into serving bowls and add a dollop of yoghurt.

6.2g fat, 17.9g net carbohydrates, 4g fibre, 7.1g protein per serving

ROASTED TOMATO SOUP

I initially used balsamic vinegar in this recipe as it gives a nice flavour, but I have tried Sukrin Gold here as this gives a slightly caramelised taste. You can opt for either or omit altogether. Remember sun-dried tomato paste may contain sugar, but you can find my own recipe in *The Pantry* chapter.

Serves 6

1kg tomatoes, quartered

1 large red onion, quartered

2–3 cloves of garlic, peeled

1 red pepper, quartered

1 carrot, cut into batons

1–2 sprigs of thyme

2 tbsp olive oil

1 tbsp Sukrin Gold or balsamic vinegar (optional)

seasoning to taste

450ml vegetable stock

2–3 tbsp sugar-free sun-dried tomato purée (or see *The Pantry* chapter)

3 tbsp mascarpone

- Preheat the oven to 165°C/gas mark 3.
- Prepare the tomatoes and vegetables and place them in a roasting tray.
- Add the sprigs of thyme in between the vegetables.
- Mix the olive oil and Sukrin Gold or balsamic together and sprinkle over the vegetables.
- Season with salt and pepper to taste.

- Place in the oven for 30 minutes.

- Remove the tomatoes and vegetables from the oven and place everything, including the juice, into a saucepan ready to liquidise with a stick blender. (If you haven't got a stick blender use a liquidiser.)

- Add the stock and tomato purée. Liquidise until smooth. If you prefer a finer soup, you can put it through a sieve.

- Add the mascarpone and bring up to heat before serving.

13.1g fat, 14.5g net carbohydrates, 4.8g fibre, 3.2g protein per serving

BROCCOLI & COCONUT SOUP

This recipe was given to me by a great friend, Hannah Shine. Hannah is an excellent homeopath and naturopathic practitioner and over the years she has helped not just my clients but also my family. This is one of her family's favourite recipes and has now become one of mine.

Serves 4

1 large head of broccoli
300ml vegetable stock
400g tin of coconut milk
seasoning to taste

- Cut up the broccoli (stems as well) and place in a large saucepan. Add the vegetable stock and the coconut milk.
- Bring to the boil and simmer for about 5 minutes until the broccoli has softened.
- Season with salt and pepper to taste.
- Use a stick blender to blend until smooth before serving.

18.7g fat, 7.1g net carbohydrates, 4.9g fibre, 5.5g protein per serving

You can make this with almost any vegetables; I have made mushroom soup, asparagus soup, butternut squash soup, courgette soup, etc.

SPICED CHICKPEA SOUP

This is a lovely warming soup and is perfect when you are feeling a bit low. This recipe uses harissa paste, but please check the label as some may contain sugar.

Serves 4

1 tsp coconut oil or butter
1 red onion, finely chopped
1 red pepper, diced
1 courgette, diced
2 sticks of celery
2–3 cloves of garlic, finely chopped
3cm piece of fresh ginger, finely chopped
2 fresh chillies, finely chopped (remove seeds if you don't want it too hot)
1 tsp harissa
400g tin of chopped tomatoes
400g tin of chickpeas
450ml vegetable, chicken or bone stock (see *The Pantry* chapter)
seasoning to taste
small handful of chopped coriander to garnish

- Place the coconut oil or butter in a saucepan and heat gently on a medium heat before adding the onion, pepper, courgette, celery, garlic, ginger and chillies. Cook for 5 minutes until beginning to soften.
- Add the remaining ingredients and stir well. Leave to simmer for 10 minutes.
- Garnish with some chopped coriander before serving.

4.7g fat, 21g net carbohydrates, 6.9g fibre, 7.5g protein per serving

BROCCOLI & STILTON SOUP

This rich and filling soup is one of my favourites and perfect if you need to fill yourself up with healthy fat if you are following a low carb diet.

Serves 4

1 tsp coconut oil or butter
1 red onion, finely chopped
1 stick of celery, finely chopped
450ml vegetable, chicken or bone stock (see *The Pantry* chapter)
750g broccoli, roughly chopped
150g stilton or other blue cheese
seasoning to taste

- Place the coconut oil or butter in a saucepan on a medium heat.
- Add the onion and celery and cook until they start to soften.
- Add the stock and broccoli and cook for 10 minutes, until the broccoli is cooked.
- Add the stilton and stir well until melted. Use a stick blender to blend until smooth.
- Season to taste before serving.

16.7g fat, 10.8g net carbohydrates, 8.6g fibre, 17.7g protein per serving

TOMATO & CHILLI SOUP

Forget those awful processed cuppa soups – this is the real thing! Perfect to pop into a flask for your working lunch. This recipe includes chillies, which not only taste delicious but also help speed up your metabolism. If you don't fancy the heat, just omit the chillies – or avoid adding the seeds as this can make it much hotter!

Serves 4

2 tsp coconut oil
1 red onion, finely chopped
2 cloves of garlic, crushed
1–2 chillies
800g fresh tomatoes, peeled and finely chopped (or use 2 x 400g
    tins of chopped tomatoes)
50g sun-dried tomatoes
½ stick of celery, finely chopped
450ml water
1 heaped tsp paprika
black pepper to taste

- Place the coconut oil, onion, garlic and chillies in a saucepan and place on a medium heat. Cook for a couple of minutes to soften before adding all the remaining ingredients.

- Cook on a low heat for 20 minutes.

- Liquidise to a purée, adding more water if required.

- Serve with a drizzle of chilli oil for an extra kick.

5.3g fat, 12.8g net carbohydrates, 4.5g fibre, 2.6g protein per serving

CREAM OF MUSHROOM SOUP

Another great soup for low carb diets as it is full of satisfying fats that help keep you full. I use a combination of cultivated and wild mushrooms but feel free to use regular cultivated mushrooms if you prefer.

Serves 4

30g dried porcini mushrooms, soaked in hot water for 20–30
    minutes
2 tsp butter
1 red onion, finely chopped
1 stick of celery, finely chopped
2–3 cloves of garlic, finely chopped
400g mushrooms (mixed), diced
2 sprigs of fresh thyme
black pepper
450ml vegetable, chicken or bone stock (see *The Pantry* chapter)
250ml double cream

- Drain the porcini mushrooms.
- Place the butter in a saucepan and add all the ingredients apart from the pepper, stock and cream.
- Cook on a medium heat until the mushrooms are starting to soften.
- Add the stock, season with black pepper and stir in the cream.
- Use a stick blender to blend until smooth. Heat through before serving.

38g fat, 9.6g net carbohydrates, 3.8g fibre, 5.8g protein per serving

PEA & HAM SOUP

A quick and easy soup that is really tasty – perfect for a quick lunch or supper. Ham hock from the butcher is really cheap so if you have time, buy these, boil them and shred the meat.

Serves 4

200g frozen peas
1 red onion, finely chopped
2 tsp butter or coconut oil
150g cooked ham, chopped
300ml hot vegetable or chicken stock
300ml full fat milk
2 sticks of celery, finely chopped
8 mint leaves
seasoning to taste
2 tbsp crème fraîche

- Remove the frozen peas from the freezer so they start to defrost at room temperature.
- Place the onion and butter or coconut oil in a saucepan and cook on a medium heat until the onion starts to soften.
- Add the ham and cook for another 3–5 minutes.
- Add the hot stock, milk, frozen peas, celery, mint leaves and seasoning. Cover with a lid and cook for 10–15 minutes.
- Remove from the heat. Add the crème fraîche and use a stick blender to blend until smooth. Season to taste before serving.

15g fat, 15g net carbohydrates, 3.3g fibre, 8.3g protein per serving

CHUNKY WINTER VEGETABLE & LENTIL SOUP

A wholesome soup, perfect for a winter's day or when you fancy a filling soup. This is a great soup to use up any vegetables you may have.

Serves 6

2 tsp coconut oil or butter
1 red onion, finely chopped
1–2 cloves of garlic, crushed
1 red pepper, diced
1 carrot, diced
1 large courgette, diced
1 sweet potato, diced
1 leek, finely chopped
2 sticks of celery, diced
1 litre vegetable or chicken stock
1 bay leaf
75g red lentils
½ tsp dried parsley or small handful of chopped fresh parsley

- Remember to cut the vegetables into equal-sized pieces so you get a more even cook.
- Place the coconut oil or butter in a sauté pan.
- Add the onion, garlic and pepper and cook for a few minutes.
- Add all the remaining ingredients, bring up to a simmer and cook for 20 minutes before serving.

5.2g fat, 25g net carbohydrates, 3.9 fibre, 9.g protein per serving

7

SIDES & SALADS

You will find a range of side dishes and salads here that can help enhance your main meals.

We all need to eat more vegetables, aiming for between five and seven portions per day. Opt for a variety of colours to ensure you are getting the best range of phytonutrients and antioxidants. Salads do not have to be boring! I can eat salad every day, but it is not just a handful of leaves – think more creatively by adding some chopped sugar-snap peas or some grated carrot or beetroot. You can also add a handful of fresh herbs, some nuts and seeds or a little finely chopped chilli to add a little kick. When cooking vegetables aim to use a steamer rather than boil as this maintains their nutritional content far better. Alternatively, think about a stir-fry or even roasting some vegetables to harness a different flavour.

We can reduce our carbohydrate intake by making some simple food swaps, such as switching from white rice to brown basmati rice. If you want to go even lower (especially those on LCHF that have to be grain free), you can swap the rice for cauliflower or broccoli rice. White potatoes are very high in starch, converting to glucose quite quickly. Opt instead for sweet potatoes. You can even make a lovely mash out of cauliflower. If you love pasta, you can swap your white pasta for brown wholemeal or even spelt or vegetable pasta. I am a huge fan of the spiralizer. I love courgette spaghetti with my bolognaise (also known as Zoodles). There are many spiralizers on the market, I like a hand-held one.

CAULIFLOWER RICE

Cauliflower rice is great if you are following a low carb or grain free diet. Surprisingly, it does not taste overpoweringly like cauliflower but instead has a light flavour. The consistency is similar to couscous. I cook this in two ways: either in the microwave or by sautéing. You can also steam it. Alternatively, place whole florets on a baking tray and roast before whizzing in your food processor. You can also use broccoli.

Serves 4

1 whole cauliflower, cut into florets

- Place the florets in a food processor and pulse for a few minutes until the cauliflower resembles rice. If you don't have a processor you can grate it, but this is messy and more time consuming.

Microwave cooking:
- Place the processed cauliflower in a container, without any water.
- Cover and cook on full power for 5–8 minutes, depending on your microwave. Stir halfway through cooking.
- Fluff up with a fork and serve immediately.

Sauté cooking:
- Put a little butter or coconut oil in a sauté pan.
- Add the processed cauliflower and toss gently on a medium heat for 5–8 minutes until heated through and softened.
- Serve immediately.

  0.4g fat, 4.8g net carbohydrates, 2g fibre, 2.8g protein per serving

Whizz up a few cauliflowers at a time and place the uncooked cauliflower rice into freezer bags. You can use this from frozen, just add to the sauté pan and cook through.

CURRIED CAULIFLOWER RICE

Add a little kick to your cauliflower rice with some Indian spices. If you are using your favourite curry powder, check the ingredients to make sure there is no added sugar.

Serves 4

1 whole cauliflower
1 tbsp butter or coconut oil
1 small red onion, finely chopped
2 cloves of garlic, crushed
1 chilli, finely chopped
1 tsp turmeric
1 tbsp sugar-free curry powder (see *The Pantry* chapter)

- Cut your cauliflower into florets.
- Place the florets in a food processor and pulse for a few minutes until the cauliflower resembles rice. Alternatively, use a grater, but it is messy and more time consuming.
- Put the butter or coconut oil in a pan.
- Add the onion, garlic, chilli and spices and combine well before adding the cauliflower.
- Stir gently on a medium heat for 5–8 minutes until heated through and softened.
- Serve immediately.

3.8g fat, 6.7g net carbohydrates, 2.7g fibre, 3.4g protein per serving

LOW-CARB/GRAIN-FREE CAULIFLOWER CHEESE

You can use this basic cheese sauce recipe and create your own dishes – I love leeks in cheese sauce, especially served with roasted gammon. It is also nice with bacon, fish or with mince to make your own lasagne (I use aubergine slices instead of pasta sheets) or moussaka.

Serves 4

1 cauliflower
300ml double cream
75–100g mature cheddar, grated
½ tsp mustard powder
black pepper

- Cut your cauliflower into florets and steam until they are only just soft.

- Place the cream in a saucepan and heat gently. Once heated, add the grated cheese and mustard powder and season with black pepper. Stir on a medium-low heat until the cheese is melted, but be careful not to heat up too much or it will stick and burn.

- Once the cheese is melted, taste and adjust by adding more cheese or seasoning to suit.

- Place the cauliflower in an ovenproof dish and pour over the cheese sauce. Add some more grated cheese and place under a preheated grill until golden and bubbling.

52g fat, 6.1g net carbohydrates, 2g fibre, 10.4g protein per serving

COWBOY BAKED BEANS

Baked beans can be packed with sugar, so forget the tinned version and make this dish to impress – it is really tasty. If you fancy a smoky flavour, add a teaspoon or two of smoked paprika. This recipe uses a slow cooker but if you don't have one, cook in a large sauté pan on the hob, making sure you stir regularly. It should only take 45 minutes on a medium heat.

Serves 6

1 tsp coconut oil or olive oil
1 red onion, diced
2 cloves of garlic, roughly chopped
200g back bacon, diced
75g chorizo sausage, sliced (skin removed)
2 x 400g tins of haricot beans, drained
400g tin of chopped tomatoes
150ml water
1 tbsp tomato purée
½ tsp yeast extract
1 tsp wholegrain mustard
½ tsp ground cumin
½ tsp chilli powder
1–2 tsp smoked paprika (optional)

- If your slow cooker needs to be preheated, turn it on 15 minutes before using. Refer to your manufacturer's instructions for more information on your specific model temperatures.

- Place the oil in a sauté pan. Add the onion, garlic, bacon and chorizo and cook until they start to soften and the bacon starts to brown. Place in the slow cooker.

- Add all the remaming ingredients and combine well. Add more water if needed.

- Turn your slow cooker to low and cook gently for 6–8 hours.

- Serve on its own or as an accompaniment in the same way as you use baked beans.

- Store any leftovers in the fridge until needed.

12.7g fat, 19g net carbohydrates, 6.2g fibre, 16.5g protein per serving

SWEET POTATO WEDGES

You can also white potatoes to make these wedges. Either way, they're a much healthier alternative to processed oven chips or wedges.

Serves 4

500g sweet potatoes, washed but not peeled
1–2 tbsp melted coconut oil or olive oil
1 tsp paprika
1 tsp dried thyme
2 cloves of garlic, crushed
black pepper to taste

- Preheat the oven to 190°C/gas mark 5.
- Slice the potatoes into thick wedges.
- Place in a bowl and spray lightly with olive oil or melted coconut oil. Sprinkle with the paprika, thyme, garlic and pepper.
- Tip into a greased baking tray and spread out evenly so the wedges are not overlapping.
- Place in the oven and bake for 20 minutes. Remove and turn or shake before popping back for 10 more minutes or until golden and crisp.
- Serve immediately.

6.5g fat, 25g net carbohydrates, 3g fibre, 1.7g protein per serving

You can use sweet potatoes instead of white potatoes to make healthy chips with a wonderful orange colour. Spice them up with some crushed chillies or serve with a salsa dip.

LEEK & STILTON STUFFED CABBAGE LEAVES

This dish is surprisingly easy and a great way to use up some leftovers. I have given a vegetarian recipe here; see below for other variations.

Serves 4

butter or coconut oil
1 leek, finely chopped
100g chestnut mushrooms, quartered
black pepper
12 large cabbage leaves
75g stilton or other blue cheese, crumbled

- Put the butter or oil in a sauté pan and fry the leek for 2 minutes. Add the mushrooms and fry for 1 minute. Season with black pepper and leave to one side.

- Meanwhile, boil the cabbage leaves for 2–3 minutes to soften them slightly. Do not discard the water but save it to steam the parcels.

- Place some of the leek and mushroom mixture in the centre of each leaf, then add a sprinkle of cheese and roll into a parcel. If you need to, you can use a wooden cocktail stick to help secure the parcel.

- When all the cabbage leaves are parcelled up, place in a steamer.

- Steam for 5–10 minutes before serving.

7g fat, 6.3g net carbohydrates, 4.8g fibre, 7.4g protein per serving

NB: Here are some suggestions for variations to this recipe:

Pancetta & Gorgonzola Cheese Parcels: fry some pancetta chunks until crispy. Place this, along with chunks of gorgonzola, into your cabbage leaf before rolling into a parcel. A delicious and moreish combination!

Mozzarella, Basil and Tomato Parcels: place chunks of mozzarella, a couple of basil leaves and a few slices of tomatoes into the centre of your cabbage leaf before rolling into a parcel. Alternatively, add a dollop of sun-dried tomato paste instead of the sliced tomato.

Bolognaise Parcels: use up any leftover bolognaise mince of an alternative meal. Place in the centre of your cabbage leaf before rolling into a parcel. For added yumminess, you can sprinkle some mature cheddar or Parmesan before rolling.

Bubble and Squeak Parcels: my dad used to love bubble and squeak. Traditionally, this dish is about using up the leftovers from a roast dinner but anything goes. Chop or mash together before placing in the centre of the leaf and roll into a parcel.

WARM BEETROOT, FETA & PINE NUT SALAD

This is a lovely salad that is also really filling – the combination of roasted vegetables, feta and pine nuts is seriously good! I enjoy this on its own for lunch but it is also good as a side dish with some grilled chicken or fish.

Serves 4

2–3 beetroots, peeled and cubed
2–3 parsnips, peeled and cubed
1 sweet potato, peeled and cubed
1 tsp dried oregano
seasoning to taste
1–2 tbsp melted coconut oil or olive oil
100g seasonal salad leaves, washed
1 red onion, sliced (or small handful of spring onions, sliced)
1 red pepper, sliced
1 tsp coconut oil
50g pine nuts
100g feta cheese, crumbled

- Preheat the oven to 200°C/gas mark 6.
- Place the cubed root vegetables in a roasting tin.
- Sprinkle with oregano, sea salt, black pepper and a drizzle of melted coconut oil or olive oil.
- Place in the oven and cook for 20 minutes or until soft and sweet.
- Meanwhile, place the leaf salad in your serving dishes. Add the red onion (or spring onions) and the red pepper. Toss to ensure it is evenly distributed.
- In a small sauté pan, add 1 tsp coconut oil and the pine nuts. Toast gently until they are just starting to darken. Leave to one side.

- When the vegetables are cooked, place them in the centre of your leaf salad.
- Finish with a sprinkle of feta cheese and the toasted pine nuts.
- Serve immediately.

19.1g fat, 27g net carbohydrates, 6.7g fibre, 9.2g protein per serving

HOT COURGETTE, RED ONION, CHILLI & SPINACH SALAD

I love this dish, perfect as a side for many meals but especially fish dishes.

Serves 4

1 tsp butter or coconut oil
3–4 courgettes, cut into sticks
1 large red onion, sliced
1 red chilli, finely chopped
black pepper
100g baby leaf spinach
chilli oil

- Place the butter or coconut oil in a sauté pan on a medium heat. Add the courgettes and red onion and cook until they start to soften.
- Add the chilli and cook for another minute. Season with black pepper.
- Finally stir in the spinach, leaving it just until it starts to wilt slightly. Remove immediately and serve with a drizzle of chilli oil.

2.5g fat, 4.9g net carbohydrates, 2.7g fibre, 2.9g protein per serving

QUINOA RAINBOW SALAD

This is a beautiful-looking salad, full of vibrant colours and chopped mint. I love this topped with grilled halloumi or crumbled feta cheese.

Serves 4

300g quinoa, cooked and drained
⅓ cucumber, diced
1 carrot, grated or spiralized
¼ red cabbage, finely shredded
1 red pepper, thinly sliced
40g baby leaf spinach
8 cherry tomatoes, halved
seeds from 1 pomegranate
small handful of fresh mint leaves, roughly chopped
2 tbsp olive oil

- Place all the ingredients into a large bowl and combine well before serving.

12.6g fat, 48g net carbohydrates, 9.5g fibre, 12.6g protein per serving

For low carb/grain free, swap quinoa for cauliflower rice. 13.6g net carbohydrates, 6g fibre.

SEARED TUNA SALAD

This is my take on the salade niçoise – it is one of my favourites and if you have never had fresh tuna before, go grab some as it is really tasty. I don't add potatoes as I prefer to keep it lower in carbs, but feel free to add some steamed new potatoes if you prefer.

Serves 4

6 large eggs
50g fine green beans, cut in half
100g mixed leaf salad, washed
1 small punnet of cherry tomatoes, cut in half
½ cucumber, thickly diced
1 red onion, thinly sliced
1 avocado, diced
50g pitted olives
olive oil
4 tuna steaks
3 cloves of garlic, crushed
pinch of dried chilli flakes
2 tbsp lemon juice

Dressing
100ml extra virgin olive oil
3 tbsp white wine vinegar
2 tbsp fresh chives, finely chopped
seasoning to taste

- Place the eggs in a large pan and cover with boiling water.
- Cook for 7 minutes, but set the timer for 4 minutes.

- Meanwhile, put the mixed leaves into a large salad bowl or individual bowls.

- When the timer goes off, add the green beans to the boiling eggs and cook for a further 3 minutes (making the total 7 minutes).

- Add the tomatoes, cucumber, red onion, avocado and olives to your salad and combine.

- Remove the eggs and green beans from the heat. Drain, then run cold water over the eggs and beans. Drain the beans well. Once cooled, peel the eggs and add to the salad, along with the beans.

- Prepare your salad dressing by combining all the ingredients. Taste and adjust to your personal preference.

- Heat a sauté pan on a medium heat.

- Rub a little olive oil onto the tuna steaks before placing into your hot sauté pan.

- Add the garlic, chilli and lemon juice. Sear on each side for a minute or two, depending on thickness. They should be served pink in the middle.

- Place the steaks onto the salad, drizzle with the dressing and serve immediately.

43g fat, 6.6g net carbohydrates, 4.6g fibre, 39g protein per serving

SPIRALIZED COURGETTE & CHICKEN SALAD

This is the salad I prepare the day after a roast chicken dinner. I always buy a large chicken so I will have plenty of leftovers to create additional meals. I slice thick chunks of the breast for this salad. If you don't have any leftover chicken, you can buy cooked chicken breast or just griddle one or two to add to the salad. You need roughly 80–100g of chicken per person. If you don't have a spiralizer, you can grate your courgettes.

Serves 2

2 courgettes, spiralized
small handful of fresh mint leaves
handful of mixed leaves, washed
1 chilli, finely chopped
200g chicken breast, thickly sliced

Dressing
100ml extra virgin olive oil
zest and juice of 1 lemon
seasoning to taste

- Place the spiralized courgettes, mint and mixed leaves in your salad bowl. Combine well.
- Add the chilli and the sliced chicken breast.
- Combine the dressing ingredients in a jug. Season to taste and adjust lemon or oil depending on personal preference.
- Drizzle the dressing over the salad and toss well before serving.

52g fat, 4.4g net carbohydrates, 3.4g fibre, 28g protein per serving

FLOWER'S CAESAR SALAD

I am a big salad fan and this really has to be my absolute favourite of them all. I adore crispy bacon, chicken and avocado. Feel free to add croutons, but personally I don't think they are needed. Sometimes I replace the chicken with halloumi – the saltiness of the halloumi goes really well with bacon and avocado.

Serves 4

100g mixed leaves, washed
1 red onion, finely chopped
¼ cucumber, diced
1 avocado, diced
300g cooked chicken, shredded
200g bacon, cooked and crispy
50g Parmesan shavings

- Place the leaves in four salad bowls.
- Add the onion, cucumber and avocado.
- Add the cooked chicken and diced crispy bacon.
- Finish with Parmesan shavings.
- Serve with a generous dollop of homemade sugar-free mayonnaise (see *The Pantry* chapter).

20g fat, 4.5g net carbohydrates, 2.1g fibre, 33g protein per serving

TABBOULEH

This is my version of the Middle Eastern dish. It is really easy to make and adds a nice touch of spice to your salad dishes. You do need to use fresh herbs in this dish – mint and parsley.

Serves 4

140g bulgur wheat
600ml hot water
3–4 tomatoes, diced
1 carrot, grated
1 red onion, finely diced
1–2 chillies, chopped
large handful of fresh mint, roughly chopped
large handful of fresh parsley, roughly chopped
zest and juice of 1 lemon
2 tsp ground sumac
2 tbsp olive oil
seasoning to taste
seeds from 1 pomegranate

- Rinse the bulgur wheat in cold water, drain and place in a pan.
- Cover the bulgur wheat with the hot water and simmer on a medium-low heat for 10 minutes, watching carefully as you want it to absorb the water to become light and fluffy but not to stick to the base of the pan.
- Drain off any excess water and place in a large salad bowl.
- Add the tomatoes, carrot, onion, chilli and fresh herbs and combine well.
- In a small jug, combine the lemon zest and juice, sumac and olive oil. Season with salt and black pepper.

- When ready to serve, pour the dressing over the bulgur salad. Combine well and finish with the beautiful pomegranate seeds.

7.7g fat, 38g net carbohydrates, 6.6g fibre, 6.2g protein per serving

For low carb/grain free, swap the bulgur wheat for cauliflower rice. 17.3g net carbohydrates, 6.1g fibre.

HOT GREEN SALAD

This is my fall-back green salad when I am a bit fed up with cold salads. If I am feeling in need of a bit more comfort, I will crumble some feta over the top along with the walnuts.

Serves 4

150g green beans
150g asparagus
150g tenderstem broccoli
1 tsp coconut oil
75g walnuts

Dressing
4 tbsp extra virgin olive oil
3 tbsp white wine vinegar
½ tsp dried mint
seasoning to taste

- Steam the vegetables lightly for 5 minutes until tender. If you don't have a steamer, blanch them in boiling water for no more than 4 minutes. You want to the vegetables to be slightly crunchy, not soft and soggy.

- Meanwhile, make the dressing by combining all the ingredients with salt and pepper, adjusting to suit your own personal taste.

- Place a little coconut oil in a small sauté pan. Add the walnuts and toss gently in the hot oil until they darken slightly. Remove and leave to one side until the vegetables are cooked.

- Place the steamed vegetables in a bowl, add the walnuts and pour on the dressing. Combine well before serving.

26g fat, 3.9g net carbohydrates, 4.6g fibre, 6.4g protein per serving

8

MAIN MEALS

SOME people have asked me why we are including main meals in a sugar-free book – surely it should just apply to sweet foods and treats? You will be surprised how much sugar is lurking in your main meal, especially if you are used to using jars of sauces.

Food manufacturers add sugar into almost everything, from gravy and stock cubes right through to ready meals, jars of sauces and condiments. You will even find sugar in your blended herb and spice mixes. Making your food from scratch, using all fresh ingredients, leaves you in control, ensuring you have the best nutritional values in your food. One of the biggest objections I come across regarding cooking from scratch is time and cost. Believe me when I say cooking from scratch, using everyday and seasonal ingredients, really does not cost a lot. I also advise batch cooking, doubling up the recipe and placing the remainder in the freezer for another meal, or as individual portions, creating your own home-made ready meals. If you are serious about sugar-free, you may also want to reduce your carbohydrate intake, especially if you are aiming to maintain a balanced blood sugar. The recipes in this chapter can all be made very low carb, so are suitable for anyone on a low-carb or low-carb high-fat diet.

MUSHROOM & CASHEW NUT ROAST

This is a fantastic recipe for a roast or Christmas dinner. Popular with meat eaters and vegetarians, it also makes a good vegan option. It does really speed up the preparation process if you have a food processor.

Serves 6

1 red large onion, finely chopped
coconut oil, for frying
200g cashew nuts, chopped
250g mushrooms, chopped
2 tsp yeast extract
50g wholemeal breadcrumbs

- Preheat the oven to 190°C/gas mark 5. Line a large loaf tin with baking parchment.
- Fry the onion in oil until translucent.
- Add the nuts and mushrooms and cook for 5 minutes.
- Add the yeast extract, followed by the breadcrumbs.
- Place into the lined loaf tin and press down firmly.
- Bake in the oven for 40 minutes (or freeze and bake when needed).

16.3g fat, 14.8g net carbohydrates, 2.3g fibre, 8.8g protein per serving

For low carb you may want to swap cashew nuts for another nut such as brazil and use 25g almond or coconut flour instead of breadcrumbs. Nutritional values using brazil nuts and almond flour are 4.8g carbohydrates, 4.4g fibre.

HEALTHY SPAGHETTI BOLOGNAISE

I think it is important to keep to traditional family favourites. Food is not just about taste; it is also about satisfying the mind.

Serves 6

1 tsp coconut oil
1 red large onion, finely chopped
2–3 cloves of garlic, finely chopped
1 red pepper, finely chopped
100g lardons or pancetta (optional)
400g beef mince
200ml beef stock or red wine
400g tin of chopped tomatoes
2–3 tsp tomato paste
1 carrot, grated
75g mushrooms, chopped
2 tsp dried oregano
black pepper

- Add the coconut oil to a sauté pan and fry the onion until soft.
- Add the garlic and pepper and cook for another couple of minutes.
- Add the lardons and mince and cook until browned. Add the stock or wine and cook for 2 more minutes.
- Add the tomatoes and tomato paste. Stir well. Add the grated carrot, mushrooms and oregano and season with black pepper. Leave to simmer very gently for 15 minutes.
- Serve on a bed of cooked wholemeal spaghetti or courgette spaghetti.

12.7g fat, 11.6g net carbohydrates, 3.4g fibre, 22g protein per serving

BEEF STROGANOFF

This is a family favourite. I featured this recipe in one of my other books and a reviewer said it was better than Jamie Oliver's – praise indeed. I will leave you to decide on that one!

Serves 4

Coconut oil or butter for frying
1 large red onion, finely chopped
2–3 cloves of garlic, crushed
500g lean beef steak chunks
300g mushrooms, sliced
2–3 tsp paprika
2–3 tsp Dijon mustard
200ml white wine
2 tsp chopped fresh tarragon
200ml double cream
Seasoning to taste

- In a large sauté pan, add the coconut oil or butter and cook the onion and garlic for 1 minute. Add the beef and cook for 3–4 minutes, stirring to ensure it is evenly browned.

- Add the mushrooms, paprika and mustard; stir well, then add the wine. Some of this will evaporate as you continue to cook for a couple of minutes.

- Add the tarragon and cook for 2–3 minutes more.

- Just before serving, stir in the double cream to form a creamy sauce and season to taste, heating through until bubbling. Serve on a bed of rice or cauliflower rice.

35g fat, 6.5g net carbohydrates, 1.8g fibre, 31g protein per serving

SALMON FISH CAKES

A really simple but tasty fish cake. You can use tinned salmon if you prefer, though fresh is far tastier. Adding omega rich oily fish will decrease the production of inflammatory proteins so has great anti-inflammatory properties.

Serves 4

2 sweet potatoes
400g salmon fillets
juice of half a lemon
black pepper
3–4 spring onions, very finely chopped
2 tsp each of chopped fresh dill and tarragon
1 egg, beaten
olive oil or coconut oil, for frying

- Cut the potatoes into chunks. Steam until soft – about 10 minutes – then mash.
- Season the salmon fillets with some of the lemon juice and black pepper. Pop under the grill and cook for 5–6 minutes. They are cooked when they flake when touched with a fork.
- Combine the fish, potato, spring onions, lemon juice and herbs together in a bowl. Season to taste. Add the egg to bind.
- Form the mixture into four cakes, place on baking parchment and chill in the fridge for 10 minutes or until needed.
- Remove from the fridge, brush with a light coating of olive oil and grill on both sides until browned, or spray a sauté pan with coconut or olive oil, and fry gently until browned on both sides.
- Serve with a green salad.

17g fat, 46g net carbohydrates, 5.4g fibre, 25g protein per serving

For low carb, swap the potatoes for mashed cauliflower and add 1 tbsp coconut flour. 6.2g carbohydrates, 4g fibre.

SPICY MEATBALLS

Kids love these and you can make them in advance and freeze – ready to pop out for a quick and easy meal.

Makes 12 meatballs

400g beef mince
1 red onion, chopped very finely
1 egg, beaten
3 tsp paprika
1–2 fresh chillies, finely chopped (optional)
1 tsp chilli powder (or more if you like them spicy)
2 tsp dried parsley
2 tsp dried oregano
seasoning to taste
coconut or olive oil for frying

- Simply combine all the ingredients together in a bowl, season and mix thoroughly.

- Form into small balls and place on a baking tray. Cover the balls with cling film and refrigerate for 30 minutes.

- Alternatively, you can freeze the balls. I normally place the baking tray in the freezer until the meatballs are firm, then take them off the tray and place in a freezer bag. This way they won't stick together and you can pull out meatballs as and when you need them.

- When you are ready to cook them, fry lightly in coconut or olive oil until browned and cooked through. Serve with homemade sugar-free tomato sauce (see *The Pantry* chapter), on a bed of wholemeal or courgette spaghetti.

2.4g fat, 1.1g net carbohydrates, 0.8g fibre, 9.8g protein per meatball

GOLDEN SALMON FILLETS

You can use any fish fillet for this but I prefer salmon. Speak to your fishmonger for the best deals.

Serves 4

60g polenta
1 tbsp chopped fresh chives
1 tbsp chopped fresh parsley
2 tbsp grated Parmesan cheese
zest of 1 lemon
seasoning to taste
4 salmon fillets
100g cream cheese

- Preheat the oven to 180°C/gas mark 4. Grease a baking tray, or line with baking parchment.
- Place the polenta, chives, parsley, Parmesan and lemon zest in a bowl, season and combine well.
- Cover the tops and sides of the fish fillets with cream cheese.
- Dip into the polenta mixture, ensuring they are well covered, and then place on the prepared baking tray.
- Bake in the oven for 10–15 minutes.
- Serve with salad.

24g fat, 7.9g net carbohydrates, 1.2g fibre, 25g protein per serving

For low carb/grain free, swap the polenta for almond or coconut flour. For added crunch, you can whizz up some pork scratchings in your food processor and use this for a coating.

CHILLI CON CARNE

This chilli can be made in advance and frozen. Chilli always improves with age so double up and make use of any leftovers.

Serves 6

olive oil, for frying
1 red onion, finely chopped
1 star anise
1 red pepper, diced
2 cloves of garlic, crushed
1 stick of celery, finely diced
1–2 chillies, chopped (depending on desired flavour)
150g chorizo, chopped (optional)
400g beef mince
400g tin of chopped tomatoes
400g tin of red kidney beans, drained
75g mushrooms, quartered (optional)
1–2 tsp chilli powder (depending on desired flavour)
2 tsp paprika
1 tsp ground cumin
2 tsp dried marjoram
3 tbsp beef bone stock (see *The Pantry* chapter) or 1 tsp sugar-free
    beef bouillon powder
2 tbsp tomato purée or homemade sun-dried tomato paste (see *The
    Pantry* chapter)
2 squares of dark chocolate (at least 80 per cent cocoa) or cacao
seasoning to taste
fresh coriander leaves

- Add a little olive oil into a pan and cook the onion and star anise until the onion starts to soften.

- Remove the star anise and add the pepper, garlic and celery and cook for 5 minutes, stirring regularly.

- Add the chopped chillies and chorizo and cook for 2 more minutes.

- Add the mince and cook until browned.

- Add the tinned tomatoes. Half fill the tin with water and swirl around, then add this to the mince.

- Add the red kidney beans, mushrooms and the remaining herbs, spices, stock a bouillon, tomato purée and dark chocolate. Season to taste.

- Allow to simmer gently for 20 minutes. The longer this is cooked, the thicker it will go. If it is too thick, you can add more water.

- Serve on a bed of rice (ideally brown), or for low carb, opt for cauliflower rice (see page 78) or Parmesan tacos (opposite).

12.7g fat, 16.2g net carbohydrates, 7.1g fibre, 26g protein per serving

For low carb, omit the kidney beans and serve with cauliflower rice or Parmesan tacos (see recipe opposite). Nutritional values without kidney beans are 10.4g carbohydrates, 3.7g fibre.

PARMESAN TACOS

The instructions below are for the microwave – you can make these in the oven, but be careful they don't burn!

- To make each taco, place 2–4 tbsp of grated Parmesan on a sheet of greaseproof paper and spread evenly to form a circle.

- Pop into the microwave and cook on high for 1–2 minutes depending on the power of your oven (start with 1 minute and then cook for 20 seconds at a time until golden – don't overcook).

- The Parmesan will melt and bubble – it is done when it has gone slightly golden.

- Remove from the microwave, but keep on the greaseproof paper and immediately place over the side of a bottle or rolling pin, pulling the sides down in order to create the taco shape. Leave until it cools and it will set into shape. Alternatively, you can place into a bowl to form your own Parmesan bowl.

FILLET OF SOLE WITH SUNNY TOMATO RELISH

The relish can be made in advance and stored in the fridge until needed; this really enhances the flavour. The fish is cooked very quickly. If you can't get any sole, ask your fishmonger for good alternatives.

Serves 4

2 tsp butter
4 sole fillets
juice of 1 lemon
salt

Tomato relish
3 tomatoes, diced
6 sun-dried tomatoes, diced
4 spring onions, finely chopped
2 cloves of garlic, crushed
1 chilli, finely chopped
small handful of fresh parsley
small handful of fresh chives
3 tbsp extra virgin olive oil
2 tbsp white wine vinegar
black pepper

- To make the relish, place all the vegetables and herbs in a bowl and combine. Mix the oil and white wine vinegar together and season with black pepper. Pour this over the vegetables and herbs, combine well and place in the fridge until needed.

- When ready to cook the fish, add the butter to a large sauté pan (you may need to make this in two batches if your pan is not big enough).

- Once the butter is melted, add the fillets. Drizzle with lemon juice and cook for 3–4 minutes on each side, adding more lemon juice and a little salt as you turn.

- Place on your plate immediately and top with any remaining lemony butter from the pan, before spooning on the tomato relish.

- Serve with a green salad.

14.3g fat, 6.5g net carbohydrates, 2.4g fibre, 18.1g protein per serving

MOUSSAKA

Traditionally this is made with lamb mince but beef works well, too.

Serves 4

2–3 aubergines, sliced
1 red onion, finely chopped
2 cloves of garlic, crushed
olive oil, for frying
400g lamb mince
400g tin of chopped tomatoes
3 tsp tomato purée
2 tsp ground cinnamon
2 tsp dried mint
300ml full fat crème fraîche or double cream
50g Parmesan, grated
seasoning to taste

- Preheat the oven to 180°C/gas mark 4.
- Place the aubergines on some kitchen paper and sprinkle with a little salt. Leave to one side.
- Meanwhile, in a sauté pan, cook the onion and garlic in a little of the olive oil. Add the lamb mince and cook until browned.
- Add the tomatoes and purée, cinnamon and mint and cook for another 2–3 minutes. Season to taste.
- Place the aubergine slices in a sauté pan with a little oil. Fry for 2 minutes, drain and leave to one side.
- Place a layer of mince in an ovenproof dish, followed by a layer of aubergines. Finish with a layer of mince.

- Finally, mix the crème fraîche with most of the grated cheese and pour over the mince. Add a sprinkle of Parmesan before placing in the oven for 30–40 minutes.
- Serve with a green salad.

32g fat, 8g net carbohydrates, 2.3g fibre, 18.9g protein per serving

STUFFED TENDERLOIN OF PORK

A great family roast; serve with roast potatoes, vegetables and home-made gravy. (See end of recipe for grain-free options.)

Serves 6

75g wholemeal breadcrumbs
1 red onion, finely chopped
2–3 cloves of garlic, finely chopped
150g lardons or pancetta
50g pine nuts
80g baby leaf spinach
6 sun-dried tomatoes (in oil), chopped
handful of fresh herbs (sage, thyme, oregano or parsley), chopped
seasoning to taste
700g pork tenderloin, butterflied and pounded flat
1–2 tbsp olive oil
sea salt

- Preheat the oven to 200°C/gas mark 6.
- In a mixing bowl, combine the breadcrumbs, onion, garlic, bacon, pine nuts, spinach, sun-dried tomatoes and chopped herbs. Mix well and season to taste.
- Place the stuffing on the meat and roll tightly. Use water-soaked string to tie the loin securely.
- Rub the skin with olive oil and sprinkle with sea salt and black pepper.
- Place the loin in a roasting tray and place in the oven. After 20 minutes, turn the oven down to 180°C/gas mark 4 and cook for a further 20–25 minutes. If it starts to darken too much while it is cooking, cover securely with foil.

- Use a meat thermometer to check if the meat is cooked, or check the juices – if they are running clear, it should be cooked.

- Remove from the oven and cover loosely with foil. Leave to rest for 10–15 minutes before carving.

- Serve with seasonal steamed vegetables.

39g fat, 13.2g net carbohydrates, 2g fibre, 27g protein per serving

For low carb, swap the breadcrumbs for 40g ground almonds or crushed pork scratchings with 2 tbsp full fat cream cheese. 5.2g net carbohydrates, 2.5g fibre.

CHORIZO CHICKEN POT

I love the flavour of chorizo, and combining it with chicken and sun-dried tomatoes is heaven. I eat this with steamed vegetables (cavolo nero is my absolute favourite). This recipe also works really well in the slow cooker – brown the chicken first before adding the rest of the ingredients.

Serves 6

1 tsp coconut oil
2 red onions, chopped
2–3 cloves of garlic, roughly chopped
2 peppers, sliced
200g chorizo sausages, sliced
500g chicken pieces (breast, leg or thigh)
2 tbsp paprika
400ml chicken stock
400g tin of chopped tomatoes
3 tsp homemade sun-dried tomato paste (see *The Pantry* chapter)
   or tomato purée
1 tsp dried oregano
½ tsp dried marjoram
small handful of chopped parsley
30g pitted olives (optional)
seasoning to taste

- Preheat the oven to 180°C/gas mark 4.
- Place the coconut oil in a sauté pan or flameproof casserole and melt on a medium heat. (I use a stock pot that can transfer to the oven.)
- Add the onions, garlic, peppers and chorizo and cook for 5 minutes.

- Add the chicken pieces and brown all over.

- Add all the remaining ingredients, season to taste and simmer gently for 5 minutes.

- Remove from the heat and place into an ovenproof dish. Cover with a lid or foil and cook for 25 minutes.

- Serve with steamed green vegetables.

12.2g fat, 11.5g net carbohydrates, 4.2g fibre, 30g protein per serving

BAKED SALMON WITH SALSA

I recently worked with a company called Cardiomato and had to create a three-course meal for journalists – in an hour – to promote heart health. This was my main dish (alongside a lovely green salad). It was a real hit so I hope you like it.

Serves 4

olive oil
2 large tomatoes, sliced
handful of basil leaves
4 salmon fillets
seasoning to taste
juice of 1 lemon

Salsa
½ cucumber, diced
4 tomatoes, diced
1 red pepper, diced
1 red onion, diced
1–2 chillies, finely chopped
small handful of coriander leaves, finely chopped
juice of 1 lemon
2 tbsp extra virgin olive oil

- Preheat the oven to 180°C/gas mark 4.
- Cut some baking parchment or foil into two large squares, big enough to wrap two salmon pieces in each parcel. Oil the centre of each well.
- Place one sliced tomato and a couple of basil leaves in the centre of each of the squares.

- Place two pieces of salmon on top of the tomatoes before seasoning with black pepper and salt to taste.

- Drizzle with lemon juice and a dash of olive oil.

- Seal the parcels and place on a baking tray.

- Bake for 20 minutes.

- Meanwhile, prepare the salsa (and the green salad).

- Place the diced vegetables and chillies in a bowl, add the coriander leaves, lemon juice and olive oil and combine well.

- Remove the salmon parcels from the oven and serve with the salsa and green salad.

31g fat, 8.1g net carbohydrates, 2.9g fibre, 23g protein per serving

CHICKEN SCHNITZEL

If you are feeling a bit stressed, grab your rolling pin and bash some chicken breasts to make these tasty schnitzels. Kids love them.

Serves 4

4 chicken breasts
50g wholemeal breadcrumbs
50g Parmesan, grated
1 tsp paprika
1 tsp dried parsley
½ tsp dried oregano
seasoning to taste
1 egg, beaten

- Here is the fun bit. Place the chicken breasts on a board, butterfly them if you wish, and use a tenderising hammer or rolling pin to bash the chicken until it is evenly flattened. You may want to cut it into smaller pieces, especially if you are serving to children.

- In a bowl, mix the breadcrumbs, Parmesan, paprika, parsley and oregano together. Season well to taste.

- Place the beaten egg in another bowl.

- Dip the chicken into the egg to coat evenly before coating in the breadcrumb mixture.

- I prefer to fry in a sauté pan with a little coconut oil or butter, but you can also oven cook (180°C/gas mark 4 for 20 minutes).

- Serve with salad or potato wedges and Cowboy Baked Beans (see page 82).

6.6g fat, 9.1g net carbohydrates, 1.2g fibre, 32g protein per serving

For low carb/grain free or gluten free, omit the breadcrumbs. For gluten free use polenta, or for low carb try almond flour or crushed pork scratchings. Nutritional values using almond flour are 1g carbohydrates, 2.5g fibre.

COTTAGE PIE

Kids love this and you can add lots of veggies in the beef mixture and the topping. This recipe can be frozen before baking.

Serves 6

1 tsp coconut oil

1 red onion, chopped

2 cloves of garlic, finely chopped

400g beef mince

1–2 sticks of celery, diced

1 carrot, diced

75g mushrooms, diced

2 tsp yeast extract (make sure it is sugar-free)

1 tbsp tomato purée

200ml beef bone broth (see *The Pantry* chapter) or stock

1–2 bay leaves

2 thyme sprigs

1 tsp paprika

seasoning to taste

Topping

2 large potatoes, cut into rough chunks

2 sweet potatoes, thickly diced

1 carrot, thickly diced

25g butter

100g mature cheddar, grated

- Preheat the oven to 180°C/gas mark 4.

- To make the topping, place the potatoes and carrots in a steamer and cook until soft.

- Meanwhile, heat the coconut oil in a large sauté pan and fry the onion for 1–2 minutes before adding the garlic and the mince. Cook, stiring, until browned.

- Add the celery, carrot and mushrooms.

- Dissolve the yeast extract and tomato purée in the stock before adding to the mince. Add the bay leaves, thyme and paprika and season well.

- Simmer for 20 minutes until tender and reduced to the desired consistency.

- Mash the steamed potatoes and carrots together. Add the butter and two thirds of the cheddar. Mix thoroughly and season to taste.

- Place the mince in a deep ovenproof dish and spoon the mash over the top. Be careful not to overfill the dish. Press the mash down gently with a fork. Top with the remaining grated cheese and a sprinkle of paprika.

- Place in the oven for 20–25 minutes until golden.

- Serve with seasonal steamed vegetables.

15.8g fat, 35g net carbohydrates, 5.3g fibre, 25g protein per serving

For low carb you can dramatically cut the carbs by opting for a cauliflower mash. Use one head of cauliflower and mash with butter or cream. 6.9g carbohydrates, 2.4g fibre.

MOROCCAN CHICKEN TAGINE

I love using spices to create new dishes – this recipe uses a lot of spices, but don't let that put you off, and don't opt for a ready-made Moroccan mix as it may contain sugar. Allow the spices to infuse and the taste is amazing.

Serves 6

400g chicken (thigh, legs or breast), diced

2 tbsp coconut oil, melted

2.5cm piece of fresh ginger, finely chopped

2 tsp paprika

1 tsp ground cumin

2 tsp turmeric

1 tsp ground cinnamon

½ tsp ground ginger

small handful of mint leaves

small handful of coriander leaves

1 chilli, finely diced

1 tbsp olive oil

1 large red onion, sliced

2 cloves of garlic, roughly chopped

1 green pepper, thickly diced

1 sweet potato, peeled and cut into chunks

1 carrot, diced

60g green beans

400g tin of chickpeas, drained

400g tin of chopped tomatoes

300ml chicken or bone stock (see *The Pantry* chapter)

- Place the chicken in a bowl.

- In a food processor place the melted coconut oil, the spices, chilli, half the chopped herbs and the tomatoes. Whizz to form a marinade.

- Pour this onto the chicken and cover with cling film. Leave to marinate in a fridge overnight or for at least 2 hours. When you are ready to cook, bring it back up to room temperature for at least 1 hour.

- Place the olive oil in a sauté pan on a medium heat. Add the onion, garlic and pepper and cook for 3–5 minutes before adding the chicken, holding back most of the marinade.

- Cook for 5 minutes and then add all the other ingredients, including the marinade and the remaining herbs.

- Cook on a low heat, simmering very gently, for 20 minutes.

- Serve with couscous or quinoa or, for low carb, opt for cauliflower rice.

8.9g fat, 23g net carbohydrates, 5.6g fibre, 23g protein per serving

For low carb, omit the chickpeas, sweet potatoes and carrot. 8.7g carbohydrates, 2.6g fibre.

RATATOUILLE WITH HALLOUMI

This is a match made in heaven – I love the saltiness of the halloumi against the sweetness of the soft vegetables. If you don't like halloumi, you can top with some crumbled feta or goats cheese.

I make up a batch of ratatouille and keep it in the freezer, ready to heat up for a fast meal when I am busy. If you want to do this, follow the recipe below but only cook for a few minutes so the vegetables remain firm; that way you won't end up with a soggy mess when you reheat.

Serves 6

2 tsp coconut oil or butter

2 red onions, sliced

2–3 cloves of garlic, roughly chopped

1 red pepper, thickly diced

1 yellow pepper, thickly diced

2 courgettes, thickly diced

1 aubergine, thickly diced

6 tomatoes, thickly diced (or a 400g tin of chopped tomatoes)

2 tbsp sun-dried tomato paste (see *The Pantry* chapter) or tomato
    purée

1 tsp dried oregano (or small handful of fresh, finely chopped)

1 tsp dried parsley (or small handful of fresh, finely chopped)

½ tsp paprika

seasoning to taste

500g halloumi (2 × 250g) packs, sliced

- In a deep pan, gently melt the coconut oil or butter before adding the onions, garlic and peppers. Cook for 2 minutes.

- Add the courgettes and aubergine and soften before adding the tomatoes, tomato paste, herbs and paprika. Season to taste.

- Cook gently on the hob for 5 minutes until the vegetables soften – don't overcook as there is nothing worse than a slimy ratatouille.

- Meanwhile, heat a little more coconut oil or butter in a sauté or griddle pan.

- Add the halloumi slices and cook on both sides until golden.

- Remove the ratatouille from the heat, place in bowls and top with the halloumi slices. Serve immediately.

23g fat, 13.4g net carbohydrates, 4.4g fibre, 24g protein per serving

ITALIAN STUFFED CHICKEN BREAST

This is my son's favourite; if your children like pizza they will love this.

Serves 4

4 chicken breasts
4 tbsp tomato purée or homemade sun-dried tomato paste (see *The Pantry* chapter)
1 red onion, finely sliced
4–8 slices of ham or pepperoni
handful of baby leaf spinach
100g cheese, grated
2 tsp oregano
seasoning to taste

- Preheat the oven to 180°C/gas mark 4.
- Cut the chicken breasts almost in half, creating a pocket so you can stuff the chicken.
- Spread the inside of the chicken with tomato purée, then add some onion, ham or pepperoni and baby leaf spinach. Finish with a little cheese.
- Place the breasts in a baking dish, ideally so they are touching.
- Spread the tops of the chicken breasts with tomato purée and finish with cheese. Add the oregano and season to taste.
- Bake in the oven for 25–30 minutes until the chicken is cooked.
- Serve with a green salad.

13.4g fat, 6.1g net carbohydrates, 2g fibre, 34g protein per serving

9

HEALTHY BBQ

WHEN it is barbecue season, we can all be tempted to eat more processed foods, but you don't have to. You can create your own fantastic recipes, giving family favourites a healthy twist. Serve with bowls of salads and dips. If you fancy savoury nibbles, you can make your own flavoured nuts, or kale or Parmesan crisps (see *The Pantry* chapter).

CHICKEN BURGERS

Why not try turkey mince for a healthier alternative to chicken.

Makes 8 burgers

1 large red onion, chopped
1–2 cloves of garlic, crushed
1 stick of celery, chopped
½ yellow pepper, chopped
500g chicken or turkey mince
30g pine nuts
seasoning to taste
1 egg, beaten (optional)

- Place all the ingredients (except the egg) in a bowl and combine well. If you prefer a smoother texture, you can add the ingredients to a food processor and mix thoroughly.

- When mixed, form into balls – these should be firm but moist. If the mixture is dry, add some beaten egg.

- Use the palm of your hand to flatten the balls into burger shapes.

- You can place the burgers in the fridge until you are ready to use them, or freeze them in layers (separate each layer with baking parchment to prevent them sticking together).

- When you are ready to cook the burgers, you can barbecue, grill, oven cook or fry them until cooked through.

- Serve with wholemeal baps, a salad garnish and a dollop of mayonnaise.

3.4g fat, 3.1g net carbohydrates, 0.7g fibre, 16.1g protein per burger

BEEF BURGERS

These are traditional beef burgers, so easy to make and far tastier than shop-bought varieties.

Makes 6 burgers

1 onion, finely chopped
1 clove of garlic, crushed
400g lean beef mince
seasoning to taste
1 egg, beaten (optional)

- Put the onion and garlic into a large bowl and stir well. Add the beef and seasoning and mix thoroughly.
- Add some of the beaten egg – if needed. Season to taste.
- Mix thoroughly and form into balls – these should be firm but moist.
- Use the palm of your hand to flatten the balls into burger shapes.
- You can place them in the fridge until you are ready to use them, or freeze them in layers (separate the layers with baking parchment to prevent the burgers sticking together).
- Barbecue, grill, oven cook or fry until cooked through.
- Garnish with salad and serve with wholemeal baps.

Variation: If you like your burgers slightly spicy, why not add some chopped chillies, coriander, cumin and paprika to the ingredients before mixing. For an added boost, add some chopped smoky bacon.

3.7g fat, 3.1g net carbohydrates, 0.4g fibre, 16.3g protein per burger

MOROCCAN STYLE KEBABS

Kebabs can be made in advance – these certainly benefit from marinating for a number of hours before cooking. I have filled with onions but you can add whatever you fancy.

Makes 8 kebabs

2 chillies (remove seeds if you don't want it too hot)
2 cloves of garlic
2 tsp paprika
1 tsp ground cumin
1 tsp turmeric
2 tsp ground cinnamon
1 tsp allspice
1 tsp ground cardamom
1 tsp ground ginger
black pepper
small handful of fresh coriander
2 tbsp olive oil
400g lamb loin, diced
3 red onions, cut into wedges

- Place all the spices, coriander and olive oil in a food processor and whizz to form a paste.
- Place the diced lamb in a freezer bag and pour in the spice paste. Secure and place in the fridge for 3–4 hours or overnight. If you are using wooden skewers, leave these to soak in water.
- When ready to cook, bring the lamb up to room temperature.
- Thread the lamb and onion wedges onto the skewers. Do not discard the remaining paste.

- Place the kebabs on the barbecue and turn regularly until evenly cooked, brushing with the spice paste as they cook.

16.7g fat, 5.1g net carbohydrates, 1.2g fibre, 9.4g protein per kebab

CHILLI & LEMONGRASS CHICKEN KEBABS

This is a great simple supper if you want to plan ahead and enjoy some free time away from the kitchen. Marinate the chicken overnight or for a few hours before needed.

Makes 8 kebabs

1 lemongrass stalk
1–2 chillies (remove the seeds if you don't want it too hot)
2–3 cloves of garlic
2cm piece of fresh ginger
small handful of coriander leaves
2 tbsp olive oil
juice and zest of 1 lime
500g chicken (4 breasts), diced

- If you have a food processor, simply add all the ingredients apart from the chicken and whizz to form a paste. If you don't have a processor, finely chop the ingredients (if you have a pestle and mortar this can help), add the oil and lime juice and zest and combine well.

- Place the mixture in a bowl or freezer bag. Add the chicken chunks and marinate overnight or for 3–4 hours. If you are using wooden skewers, leave these to soak in water.

- When ready to prepare, thread the chicken onto the skewers – you could alternate each chicken chunk with a cherry tomato, a slice of courgette or a wedge of red pepper. Place the kebabs on the barbecue and turn regularly until evenly cooked through.

- Serve with fluffed up rice or cauliflower rice and a lovely salad – perfect, yet so simple!

3.9g fat, 0.6g net carbohydrates, 0.2g fibre, 15.9g protein per kebab

MARINATED KING PRAWN SKEWERS

If you are using wooden skewers, remember to soak them for several hours before you use them to prevent them from burning.

Makes 6 skewers

18 king prawns, peeled and deveined
1–2 chillies, finely chopped
3–4 cloves of garlic, finely chopped
1 tbsp rice malt syrup (optional)
zest and juice of 1 lime
4 tbsp extra virgin olive oil
small handful of chopped parsley
black pepper

- Place the deveined prawns in a freezer bag.
- In a jug, combine all the remaining ingredients before pouring into the freezer bag with the prawns.
- Seal and combine. Leave to marinate for at least 1 hour.
- When ready to cook, thread three prawns onto each skewer. Brush with any remaining marinade before cooking on the barbecue or a hot grill for 3–4 minutes each side until done.

8.6g fat, 0.4g net carbohydrates, 0.1g fibre, 4.5g protein per skewer

10

FAST FOOD

WE have all got used to enjoying fast food whenever we fancy. This desire has worked its way into our kitchen, with food manufacturers recreating our favourite take-out meals at home. As convenient as these may appear, they are often low in nutrients and full of sugars, unhealthy fats and salt.

The idea of fast food is to be just that – fast – so fill your freezer with these recipes so you are creating your own frozen, ready meals. These will be much healthier and, in the long-run, will save you money and time.

HEALTHY SOUTHERN FRIED CHICKEN

If you love southern fried chicken, try this recipe. I first used this in a cookery class at my local school and the children and teachers went crazy for it. They were begging for the recipe. Much healthier than any shop or fast food concoction! Get your children in the kitchen and let them help you prepare it.

This is also really nice cold – makes a great option for packed lunch.

Top Tip! Why not fill an airtight jar or container with the spice mix. It will be ready for the next time you fancy this tasty dish. Simply double up the quantities!

Serves 4

1 egg, beaten
500g chicken pieces (drumstick, thigh or breast)

Spice mix
150g fine polenta
4 tsp paprika
1 tsp dried parsley
1 tsp dried oregano
½ tsp dried tarragon
1 tsp dried thyme
1 tsp garlic powder
½ tsp onion salt
½ tsp celery salt
generous seasoning of black pepper

- Preheat the oven to 190°C/gas mark 5.

- Mix all the ingredients for the spice mix, making sure it is combined evenly. Place this in a large dish.

- Place the beaten egg in a dish.

- Now for the messy bit – dip the chicken pieces into the egg, then into the spice mixture, ensuring they are evenly covered.

- To make sure the chicken crisps up evenly I place the chicken onto a cooling rack before putting this onto a baking sheet. The idea is to allow the heat and air to circulate all around the chicken, ensuring an even and crisp cook.

- Cook for 20–30 minutes depending on the size of your chicken pieces.

5.6g fat, 26g net carbohydrates, 3.8g fibre, 44g protein per serving

For low carb/grain free, use almond or coconut flour instead of polenta. You can also use crushed pork scratchings. Nutritional values using almond flour are 2.7g carbohydrates, 5.9g fibre.

TANDOORI CHICKEN

There is something deeply satisfying about flinging around herbs and spices when cooking, and it is a great way to get the family's attention as the flavours start to waft around the house.

Serves 6

1 red onion, finely chopped
2–3 cloves of garlic, crushed
1–2 chillies, finely chopped
1 tsp ground coriander
1 tsp ground cumin
3–4 tsp curry powder
2 tsp turmeric
1 tsp ground cinnamon
2–3 tsp paprika
2.5cm piece of fresh ginger, grated
juice and zest of 1 lemon
dash of olive oil or 2 tsp coconut oil
250ml coconut cream
700g chicken pieces

- Using your food processor, mix the onion, garlic and chillies with the herbs and spices, the lemon juice and zest, olive oil (or coconut oil) and coconut cream.

- Place the chicken pieces in a freezer bag and pour over the spice mixture. Tie the top and combine thoroughly. For best flavour, leave to marinate for a few hours.

- When ready to cook, preheat the oven to 200°C/gas mark 6.

- Place the chicken in a baking dish and cook for 40 minutes.

NB: If you are planning a barbecue, you can marinate the chicken for up to 24 hours until needed. Remove the chicken from the marinade, brush with oil and place on the barbecue to cook.

20g fat, 6.1g net carbohydrates, 2g fibre, 32.6g protein per serving

HEALTHY BEEF CURRY

You can use this recipe with vegetables, lamb or chicken. This uses beef, which works really well in the slow cooker.

Serves 6

1 tsp coconut oil or olive oil

1 large red onion, chopped (or 2 medium)

1 red pepper, sliced

500g beef, diced

400g tin of chopped tomatoes

200ml beef bone stock (see *The Pantry* chapter)

3 tbsp coconut cream

chopped coriander leaves

1 lime

Curry paste

3cm piece of fresh ginger, peeled

3–4 cloves of garlic

1–3 chillies, depending on personal taste

1–2 tbsp olive oil

small handful of coriander leaves

1 tbsp sugar-free garam masala (or use my sugar-free curry powder
  – see *The Pantry* chapter)

½ tsp ground cumin

2 tsp turmeric

- To make the curry paste, in a food processor, place the ginger, garlic, chilli, olive oil, coriander leaves, garam masala, cumin and turmeric. Whizz to form a paste. Leave to one side (store in the fridge or freeze until needed).

- Heat the coconut oil in a large sauté pan. Add the onion and pepper and cook for a couple of minutes.

- Add the beef and brown all over before adding the curry paste, tomatoes and stock. Simmer gently for 20–25 minutes or slow cook for 6–8 hours on high – perfect for tougher cuts of meat.

- Just before serving, stir in the coconut cream, coriander leaves and a squeeze of lime.

- Stir and serve on a bed of brown basmati or cauliflower rice.

CHICKEN FAJITA WRAPS

A quick and easy meal that can be ready in 15 minutes from start to finish. I use my own fajita seasoning, which I make in batches and store in a jar. If you like it spicy you could add some chopped fresh chilli to your seasoning before adding the chicken.

Serves 4

4 chicken breasts, cut into strips
1 tsp olive oil or coconut oil
2 peppers, sliced
½ iceberg lettuce
½ cucumber, cut into lengths
2 avocados, sliced (optional)

Fajita seasoning
2 tsp chilli powder
2 tsp garlic powder
3 tsp paprika
2 tsp dried oregano
1 tsp ground cumin
2 tsp onion powder
1 tsp dried parsley
black pepper
salt

- To make the fajita seasoning, mix all the ingredients together and store in a jar or airtight container. This can be made upto a month in advance. If you like you can double all the ingredients, ready for another quick meal.

- Place the chicken strips in a bowl and add some of the seasoning – use half the above mix if you want it mild, more if you want it with a bit more kick. Stir until it is well covered.

- Drizzle a small amount of olive oil or coconut oil in your sauté pan and heat gently.

- Add the chicken and keep it moving until it starts to turn white.

- Add the sliced peppers and continue to cook until your chicken is cooked right through – timings depend on the thickness of the chicken but should not take more than 10 minutes.

- Meanwhile, slice the iceberg lettuce and place in a bowl. Add the cucumber (I also add some avocado if I am having a very spicy fajita) and combine well.

- When the chicken is cooked, place in a serving dish.

- Check the carbohydrate content when you choose your wraps, and go for wholemeal. If you like your wraps warm, place a few at a time in a microwave for 45 seconds.

- Fill the wraps with a mixture of the salad and chicken.

17.6g fat, 7.4g net carbohydrates, 7g fibre, 43g protein per serving (without wraps)

For low carb/grain free, serve the chicken on top of the salad instead of in a wrap – I love it this way.

TASTY FISH FINGERS

These are far tastier and healthier than processed ones and can be prepared in advance and frozen. Get the kids to help you.

Makes 10 fish fingers

500g white fish fillets
200g fine polenta
1 tsp dried parsley
½ tsp onion salt
zest of ½ lemon
seasoning to taste
1 egg

- Place the fish fillets on a chopping board. Use a sharp knife to cut into thick fingers.
- Preheat the oven to 180°C/gas mark 4.
- Place the polenta in a bowl and add the parsley, onion salt, lemon zest and seasoning to taste. Combine well.
- In another bowl, beat the egg.
- Dip the fish fingers into the egg, then into the polenta mixture. Place onto a greased baking tray.
- Bake in the oven for 15–20 minutes until golden. Serve with home-made ketchup (see *The Pantry* chapter).

1.5g fat, 13.9g net carbohydrates, 1.5g fibre, 11.1g protein per fish finger

For low carb/grain free, swap the polenta for ground almonds or coconut flour. You can also use crushed pork scratchings. With ground almonds: 1.3g carbohydrates, 2.6g fibre.

LAMB KOFTAS

These spicy meatballs are great served with a variety of Indian dishes: my son likes to eat these with lentil dahl. They taste great for a packed lunch with a salad and they can even be cooked on skewers on your barbecue.

Serves 4 (makes up to 12 meatballs)

500g lamb mince
1 tsp ground cumin
1 tsp paprika
1 tsp turmeric
1 tsp ground coriander
½ tsp ground cinnamon
½ tsp chilli powder
1 chilli, finely chopped
1 red onion, very finely chopped
small handful of coriander leaves, finely chopped
seasoning to taste
2 tbsp melted coconut oil or olive oil

- Place the mince in a large bowl and break up.
- Add all the remaining ingredients apart from the oil and mix thoroughly until evenly combined.
- Form into balls and place on a tray lined with baking parchment.
- Pop into the fridge for 30 minutes to chill.
- When ready to cook, you can fry, oven cook (180°C/gas mark 4 for 15–20 minutes) or barbecue on skewers.

31g fat, 3.4g net carbohydrates, 1.3g fibre, 25g protein per serving

NUTRIENT PACKED CHICKEN CURRY

This curry is packed with vegetable goodness. This recipe uses curry powder, but please check your preferred spice blends as some may have added sugar.

Serves 4

1 large red onion, chopped
2 red peppers, sliced
100g sweet potato, diced
1 tsp coconut or olive oil
400g chicken breasts, diced
50g red lentils
200ml chicken stock or hot water
80g baby leaf spinach
3 tbsp coconut cream
chopped coriander leaves
zest of 1 lime

Spice paste
3cm piece of fresh ginger, peeled
3–4 cloves of garlic
1–2 chillies, depending on personal taste
2 tbsp olive oil
small handful of coriander leaves
1 heaped tbsp sugar-free curry powder (see *The Pantry* chapter)
6 tomatoes

- To make the spice paste, in a food processor, add the ginger, garlic, chilli, olive oil, coriander, curry powder and tomatoes. Whizz to form a paste. Leave to one side (store in the fridge or freeze until needed).

- Remember to cut the vegetables to equal size so you get a more even cook.

- Heat the oil in a sauté pan on a medium heat. Add the onion and peppers and cook for 2–3 minutes to soften before adding the chicken. Once the chicken has turned white (but still pink in the middle) add the sweet potato and lentils along with the spice paste. Add the water or chicken stock.

- Simmer gently on a low heat for 20 minutes. Five minutes before serving add the spinach, coconut cream, chopped coriander and the lime zest. The spinach leaves will need to be stirred in carefully; once they are warm they will soften completely.

- Stir well and serve alone or with cauliflower rice or brown basmati.

10.9g fat, 35g net carbohydrates, 7g fibre, 36g protein per serving

For low carb, omit the sweet potato and lentils and serve with cauliflower rice. 16.4g carbohydrates, fibre 5.1g.

HEALTHY CHICKEN KIEV

A pet hate of mine is savoury foods containing unnecessary sugar. Many shop-bought chicken Kievs contain added sugar. I like to use my own frozen garlic butter, which I store in the freezer in thick slices. Don't worry if you don't have any frozen garlic butter, you can make it with chilled butter.

Serves 4

4 chicken breasts
200g fine polenta
1 tsp dried parsley
1 tsp dried oregano
½ tsp onion salt
seasoning to taste
1 egg

Garlic butter
3–4 cloves of garlic, crushed and chopped
150g butter, softened
small handful of finely chopped parsley
zest of ½ lemon
seasoning to taste

- First, make the garlic butter. Mix the garlic, butter, parsley and lemon zest together and season to taste. Place a sheet of cling film on your worktop and plop the butter mixture into the centre. Wrap to form into a sausage shape and either freeze if making in advance, or chill in the fridge while you prepare the chicken.

- Place the polenta in a bowl and add the parsley, oregano, onion salt and season to taste. Combine well.

- In another bowl, beat the egg.

- Place the chicken onto a chopping board. Using a sharp knife, make a deep pocket into each breast, making sure you don't cut all the way through the chicken.

- Remove the garlic butter from the fridge or freezer. Cut into thick chunks and place one or two chunks into each of the chicken pockets.

- Dip the chicken into the polenta mixture, then the egg, then into the polenta mixture for the final time. You need to ensure the chicken is sealed – dipping it into the egg and polenta mixture will give a protective coating to prevent the butter leaking out. Place onto a greased baking tray. You can pop these into the fridge to chill until you are ready to cook them.

- Bake in the oven at 180°C/gas mark 4 for 20–25 minutes until golden.

35g fat, 36g net carbohydrates, 4.3g fibre, 32g protein per serving

For low carb/grain free, swap polenta for ground almonds or coconut flour. You can also use crushed pork scratchings. With ground almonds: 4.1g carbohydrates, 7.1g fibre.

LENTIL DAHL

This is so easy to make and costs very little. You can make it mild and creamy by adding some Greek yoghurt or coconut cream – ideal for children – or spice it up to suit your taste. You can also make this into a soup by adding more liquid.

Serves 4

1 red onion, chopped
2 cloves of garlic, crushed
3–5cm piece of fresh ginger, finely chopped
1 red pepper, chopped (optional)
1 tsp coconut oil or olive oil
2–3 tsp sugar-free curry powder (or use my recipe – see *The Pantry* chapter)
1–2 tsp turmeric
3 tomatoes, finely chopped
1 tbsp tomato purée
100g red lentils
300–400ml water
seasoning to taste

- In a large pan, fry onion, garlic, ginger and pepper in coconut or olive oil until soft.

- Add curry powder, turmeric, tomatoes and tomato purée and cook for another 2 minutes.

- Add lentils and cover with water. Simmer gently until the lentils have softened. Add more water if necessary. Season to taste.

3.1g fat, 23g net carbohydrates, 4.5g fibre, 8.1g protein per serving

PIZZA PIAZZA

If I have children over for a play date, I normally get them to make their own pizzas. They have a great time making the dough. I place a large piece of foil or baking parchment in front of each child. They can roll their dough straight onto the foil, which saves mess and avoids using baking trays. I normally put a variety of topping ingredients in small bowls so they can help themselves to make their own creation. Once done, I simply pick up and place straight into a hot oven and bake for 10–15 minutes.

To save time, you could make your own dough in advance. Roll it out and place on greased foil or baking parchment. Stack on top of each other, cover in cling film or foil and refrigerate until ready to use. You can also freeze these bases, layering between sheets of baking parchment and wrapping in a freezer bag.

The recipes below are for three different pizza bases: **Basic dough**, which is a standard yeast recipe; **Cauliflower base**, which is great for low carb or low calorie; and finally my adaptation of the **'Fat Head' pizza**, which is high in fat and low in carbs, made from ground almonds and cheese. This is my favourite.

> **NOTE: Please be aware of the difference in carbohydrate values between the bread dough pizza and the cauliflower and Flower's Fat Head pizza.**

BASIC PIZZA TOPPING

Pizza topping can be made using homemade pasta sauce (see *The Pantry* chapter) or even simple tomato purée mixed with olive oil and herbs. Decorate your pizza with grated cheese, mushrooms, tuna, peppers, pepperoni, chorizo or ham. Experiment and have fun.

BASIC PIZZA DOUGH

Makes 2 large pizza bases or 4 small

500g strong bread flour
325ml warm water
1 x 7g sachet of dried yeast
2 tbsp olive oil

- Sift the flour into a bowl and make a well in the centre.

- Mix the water, yeast and oil together. Pour into the middle of the flour.

- Mix thoroughly to form a dough. Transfer the dough onto a floured board and knead well until the dough springs back when pulled.

- Place in a floured bowl and cover the bowl with cling film or a warm damp cloth and leave until it has doubled in size. This takes about 1 hour.

- Knead again, then divide and roll out to form two large or four individual pizzas.

- This dough can be stored in the fridge or freezer until needed.

- When ready to cook, preheat the oven to 190°C/gas mark 5.

- Add your chosen toppings to the pizza bases and bake for 15–20 minutes.

15.5g fat, 180g net carbohydrates, 8.2g fibre, 29g protein per large pizza base

CAULIFLOWER PIZZA BASE

This is very popular with sugar-free, low carb and low calorie dieters. You can use cauliflower, broccoli or finely grated courgette for this recipe, all work well.

Makes 2 pizza bases

1 cauliflower
180g full fat cream cheese
1 egg, beaten
seasoning to taste

- Preheat the oven to 200°C/gas mark 6.

- Place your cauliflower into a food processor and whizz until it resembles couscous. If you don't have a food processor, you can grate the cauliflower.

- Put the cauliflower in a bowl and pop into the microwave for 4 minutes on high. If you prefer not to use a microwave, you can fry the cauliflower.

- When cooked, allow to cool before adding the cream cheese and egg. Mix to form a dough and season to taste. Divide the dough into two.

- Place one large sheet of baking parchment on the worktop and place the dough in the centre of the parchment. Place another sheet of parchment on top of the dough and press down with your hands. This is the easiest way to form the base without getting sticky hands and worktop.

- Press into your pizza base shape using your hands and knuckles. The dough needs to be about 1cm thick.

- Place the whole thing, including parchment, onto a baking tray before removing the top sheet of parchment. Repeat for the second base.

- Pop into the oven and cook until it starts to go golden on top.
- Remove and top with your chosen toppings before placing back into the oven for another 8–10 minutes until bubbling and golden.

25g fat, 10g net carbohydrates, 3.1g fibre, 12.7g protein per pizza base

FLOWER'S 'FAT HEAD' PIZZA

I love this pizza. It is my adaptation of the brilliant 'Fat Head Pizza' which is admired in the world of low carb. You start off making a large pizza, salivating, thinking of consuming the whole lot in one go, but despite the thin crust and innocent looks, this pizza is not for the faint-hearted. **It seriously fills you up**. I can manage two slices and then I am full, thanks to the fat content. It is also good to have cold, perfect for packed lunches and snacks. You can also freeze the bases.

Makes 2 pizza bases

250g cheddar or mozzarella cheese, grated
100g full fat cream cheese
2 eggs, beaten
200g almond flour or ground almonds
½ tsp chilli powder
½ tsp garlic powder
1 tsp dried oregano
seasoning to taste

- Preheat the oven to 200°C/gas mark 6.
- Place the cheese and cream cheese in a bowl and pop into the microwave for 1 minute to soften (this makes it easier to form into a dough).
- Remove from the microwave and add all the remaining ingredients, combining well. This will form a wet dough.
- Form into a ball and cut in half.
- Place one large sheet of baking parchment on the worktop and place a ball of dough in the centre of the parchment. Place another sheet of parchment on top of the dough and press down with your hands.

- Press into your pizza base shape using your hands and knuckles. The dough needs to be about 1cm thick.

- Place the whole thing, including parchment, onto a baking tray before removing the top sheet of parchment. Repeat for the second base.

- Pop into the oven and cook until it starts to go golden on top.

- Remove and top with your chosen toppings before placing back into the oven for another 8–10 minutes until bubbling and golden (if cooking from frozen, increase cooking time by 5–10 minutes).

117g fat, 8.6g net carbohydrates, 13.6g fibre, 63g protein per pizza base

11

JUST DESSERTS

IT is always lovely to have a special dessert after a meal but these are often packed with unnecessary sugar.

If your child likes yoghurt, opt for natural Greek yoghurt and add some fresh berries. You will still get some sugars but these will be from whole fruits and not added sugars or fruit concentrates.

RASPBERRY MOUSSE

It's a bit cheeky to call this a mousse as really it is a simple baseless cheesecake! You can use strawberries or try some blueberries with a little lemon zest. I like the flavour of raspberries so that is my absolute favourite. I don't bother with any sweetener as I like the sharpness of the raspberries combined with the smooth cream. If you don't have stevia liquid, opt instead for a teaspoon or two of xylitol or erythritol blend as powdered stevia can leave more of an aftertaste than the liquid.

Serves 4

180g cream cheese
150ml extra thick cream
2–3 tbsp Greek yoghurt
150g frozen raspberries, slightly defrosted
a few drops of liquid stevia to taste (optional)

- Put all ingredients in a bowl and beat together until well blended.
- Place in dessert glasses and place in the fridge to chill for 30 minutes before serving.

32g fat, 4.1g net carbohydrates, 2.5g fibre, 4.6g protein per serving

RHUBARB CRUMBLE

I love rhubarb – nothing nicer than picking fresh from the garden and making this delicious dessert. Rhubarb goes well with strawberries so if I have any strawberries that look like they need using up, I add them just before popping on the crumble topping. See overleaft for grain-free options.

Serves 6

650g rhubarb
75g xylitol or erythritol blend (or stevia to taste)
100ml water
140g wholemeal, spelt or rye flour
60g oats
30g mixed seeds
100g chilled butter, cut into small pieces

- Preheat the oven to 180°C/gas mark 4.
- Place your rhubarb in a saucepan and add the xylitol or stevia and water. Cook gently for 5–8 minutes to start to soften the fruit.
- Pour this into an ovenproof dish.
- In a bowl, combine the flour, oats and seeds. Add the butter and rub in until the mixture resembles breadcrumbs.
- Sprinkle this over the fruit base, making sure it is spread evenly.
- Place the crumble in the oven and cook for 20 minutes.
- Serve with cream or homemade custard (see the recipe for Rhubarb and Custard Pots in this chapter).

17.4g fat, 23g net carbohydrates, 5.7g fibre, 5.9g protein per serving

For low carb/grain free, swap the flour for coconut flour or ground almonds. Omit the oats but add some chopped nuts. 4.3g carbohydrates, 6.2g fibre.

VANILLA & BLUEBERRY DESSERT

This is a little bit like a brûlée without the sugar-coated top. You can use any berries with this; blueberries or raspberries work really well. I sometimes add a little lemon zest – this really complements the blueberries.

Serves 4

80g blueberries
200g full fat cream cheese
150ml thick cream
1 tsp sugar-free vanilla paste
1–2 tbsp xylitol or erythritol blend (or a few drops of stevia to taste) (optional)
6 eggs

- Preheat the oven to 200°C/gas mark 6.
- Divide the blueberries among four ramekin dishes.
- Combine the cream cheese, cream, vanilla paste, xylitol and eggs – I use a hand whisk or my hand blender for this.
- Pour this mixture into the ramekins.
- Boil the kettle. Place the ramekins in a deep roasting pan. Carefully pour boiling water into the roasting pan until it is about halfway up the sides of the ramekins.
- Place in the oven and bake for 30 minutes. Remove and leave to cool. I normally leave these in the fridge for 30 minutes. I add a few berries on the top before serving.

29g fat, 5.2g net carbohydrates, 0.3g fibre, 14.7g protein per serving

LOW CARB BAKED CHOCOLATE CHEESECAKE

It is really nice to have a sweet, especially when you are starting out on sugar-free. I would always opt for xylitol or erythritol – stevia is good but it can be a bit hit and miss to get the right sweetness for your palate – too much and it can leave a chemical aftertaste. Always use full fat Greek yoghurt as it keeps its shape during cooking.

NB: For a nice variation, add a few drops of mint or orange extract to the mixture to create a whole new flavour.

Serves 8

75g butter
75g ground almonds
75g hazelnuts, finely chopped
2 medium eggs, separated
50g xylitol or erythritol blend
200g cream cheese
4 tbsp extra thick cream
150g full fat Greek yoghurt
100g dark chocolate (at least 80 per cent cocoa content), plus extra grated dark chocolate to decorate

- Preheat the oven to 160°C/gas mark 3.

- Melt the butter in a saucepan. Add the ground almonds and chopped nuts and combine well. Press into a greased spring-form cake tin (approx. 22cm) and press down firmly with the back of a spoon. Place in the fridge while you complete the next phase.

- Combine the egg yolks and xylitol and beat until light and fluffy. Stir in the cream cheese, cream and yoghurt.

- Melt the dark chocolate in a bain-marie (a bowl over a saucepan of boiling water – but don't let the water touch the base of the bowl) or in a microwave (be careful not to overcook – about 30–40 seconds is often enough). Once melted, combine with the creamed mixture.

- Whisk the egg whites until they are stiff. Fold into the mixture gently. Once blended, pour this over the base. Cover with foil.

- Place the cheesecake in the oven and cook for 40 minutes. Leave to cool completely before refrigerating.

- Add some grated dark chocolate to the top before serving with some fresh raspberries and a dollop of Greek yoghurt.

36g fat, 5.9g net carbohydrates, 3.3g fibre, 9.7g protein per serving

CHOCOLATE MOUSSE

Rich in essential fatty acids but tastes like a luxury chocolate mousse – perfect!

Serves 2

1 ripe avocado
2 tbsp cocoa
75–125ml full fat milk
2 tsp rice malt syrup (or stevia drops to taste)

Optional extras (choose one)
a few drops of vanilla, orange or mint extract
1–2 tsp peanut butter
4 hazelnuts

- Place the avocado, cocoa and 75ml of the milk into a blender with your chosen flavouring and blend until smooth. Add more milk until you get your desired consistency.
- Taste as you go and add your sweetener to suit.
- Chill and serve with some fresh berries.

19.2g fat, 6.5g net carbohydrates, 7.1g fibre, 6.6g protein per serving

BAKED EGG CUSTARD

Egg custard was something my mum would always bake for me when I was feeling poorly. For me, it is comfort food, but you can make this sugar-free and low carb. I use cream and eggs, but you can use milk if you prefer. You can also use this mixture to make egg custard tarts.

Serves 2

4 eggs

200ml thick cream or full fat milk

2 tbsp xylitol or erythritol blend (or a few drops of liquid stevia to taste)

1 tsp sugar-free vanilla extract (optional)

grated nutmeg or ground cinnamon

- Preheat the oven to 180°C/gas mark 4.

- Boil the kettle so you have plenty of hot water.

- In a bowl or jug, beat the eggs with the cream or milk, sweetener and vanilla.

- Pour the mixture into ramekins. Sprinkle with nutmeg or cinnamon.

- Place the ramekins in a deep baking tray.

- Fill the tray with hot water until it comes up halfway up the ramekins.

- Place in the oven and cook for 20–25 minutes until firm.

34g fat, 3.3g net carbohydrates, 0g fibre, 17.2g protein per serving

FRESH BERRY PAVLOVA

Who says we have to give up lovely desserts when we are sugar-free? This is my absolute favourite pudding and something I would have always chosen in a restaurant before going sugar-free. This is also a great recipe to use up any egg whites. If your meringue breaks, don't worry, simply rename your dessert as an Eton Mess and crumble the meringue into a bowl, adding the cream and berries in layers.

Serves 6

4 egg whites
100g xylitol or erythritol blend
1 tsp white wine vinegar
1 tsp cornflour (optional)
300g cream or Greek yoghurt
1 tsp sugar-free vanilla extract
200g berries (I always opt for raspberries as they are my favourite)

- Preheat the oven to 200°C/gas mark 6.
- Place the egg whites in a clean bowl and whisk until glossy and forming soft peaks.
- Add the xylitol a little at a time and beat until it forms firm peaks.
- Mix in the cornflour (if using) and vinegar.
- Line a baking tray with baking parchment (you can stick this to the tray using a small dollop of the egg white mixture).
- Pipe or spoon the mixture to form one large circle of meringue
- Place in the oven and immediately turn down to 150°C/gas mark 2.
- Cook for 1 hour and turn the oven off, leaving the meringues inside to cool. Store in an airtight container until needed.

- In a bowl mix the cream or yoghurt with the vanilla extract.
- Place the meringue on a serving plate, dollop on the cream/yoghurt mixture and cover with berries.

11.9g fat, 4.2g net carbohydrates, 2.3g fibre, 4.3g protein per serving

For low carb/grain free, omit the cornflour.

SUGAR-FREE BERRY-JELLY

If you are using raspberries or strawberries, you may want to sieve to remove the seeds before adding to the liquid.

Makes 1 pint of jelly (serves 6)

120g fresh or frozen berries of your choice
500ml water
50g xylitol or erythritol blend (or a few drops of stevia liquid to
    taste)
squeeze of lemon juice to taste
4–5 tbsp powdered gelatine

- I use my Nutribullet to pulp the fruit (adding a little water to help blend) but you can use a blender or just mush together as thoroughly as you can until you have a smooth pulp.

- In a pan, heat the water, sweetener and lemon juice until combined and warm. Add the gelatine and stir with a whisk until combined and the water starts to look a bit glossy and smooth.

- Add the fruit purée and combine well before carefully placing into jelly moulds.

- Leave to set in the fridge until set.

0.1g fat, 0.9g net carbohydrates, 1.3g fibre, 6.6g protein per serving

Milk Jelly — use 200ml water to dissolve the gelatine, then add 300ml full fat milk along with the fruit purée.

VANILLA PANNA COTTA

I love creamy puddings and this is perfect to be made in advance for dinner parties. You can adjust the sweetener to taste. If you only have sheet gelatine, that is fine, just follow the manufacturer's instructions – normally soak in cold water until it becomes soft before adding to your milk.

Serves 4

2–3 tsp powdered gelatine
250ml full fat milk
250ml double cream
2 tsp sugar-free vanilla extract or paste
2–3 tbsp xylitol or erythritol blend (or stevia to taste)

- Sprinkle the gelatine over 2–3 tbsp of water and leave to one side.
- Heat the milk and cream together gently until just starting to come to a boil.
- Add the vanilla extract and sweetener.
- Remove from the heat, add the gelatine and combine.
- Pour into ramekin dishes and place in the fridge to set.
- Serve with some fresh berries.

38g fat, 4.6g net carbohydrates, 0g fibre, 12.7g protein per serving

RHUBARB & CUSTARD POTS

There is something really comforting about custard puddings. If you find rhubarb a bit tart, you can add a few strawberries as well as the xylitol or stevia to taste.

Serves 6

500g rhubarb
1–2 tbsp xylitol or erythritol blend (or stevia to taste)

Custard
450ml full fat milk
3 tbsp cornflour
3 egg yolks (keep the whites and use them to make meringues or
    freeze them)
2–3 tbsp xylitol or erythritol blend (or stevia to taste)
1 tsp sugar-free vanilla extract

- Place the rhubarb in a pan with 3–4 tbsp of water and the xylitol or stevia. Cook gently until the rhubarb softens.

- While the rhubarb is cooking, make the custard. Place the milk in a saucepan and gently bring to a simmer; do not let it boil over.

- While the milk is heating, in a large bowl, mix the cornflour, egg yolks, sweetener and vanilla extract together to form a paste.

- When the milk is starting to simmer, remove from the heat and stir very slowly into your egg yolk paste. Keep stirring until it starts to thicken. You may want to place it back into the saucepan to thicken over a low heat (not high or it will burn on the bottom). Keep stirring until it thickens. If you get lumps, beat with a balloon whisk, but if you keep it on a low heat and keep stirring you should be fine.

- Place the rhubarb in the bottom of your serving glasses. Add the custard and finish with a few more dollops of rhubarb.
- Serve hot or cold.

5.8g fat, 9.1g net carbohydrates, 2.4g fibre, 5.2g protein per serving

For low carb/grain free, swap the cornflour for coconut flour or xanthan gum.

BAKED LEMON & LIME CHEESECAKE

Serves 8

75g butter
75g ground almonds
75g hazelnuts, finely chopped
6 medium eggs
400g full fat cream cheese
300ml thick cream
80g xylitol or erythritol blend (or stevia to taste)
zest and juice of 1 lime
zest only of 2 lemons

- Preheat the oven to 150°C/gas mark 2.

- Melt the butter in a saucepan. Add the ground almonds and chopped nuts and combine well. Press into a greased spring-form cake tin (approx. 22cm) and press down firmly with the back of a spoon. Place in the fridge while you complete the next phase.

- Place the eggs in a bowl and beat with a whisk. Add the remaining ingredients and whisk well. If your lime is hard to juice, place it in the microwave for 20 seconds before juicing.

- Pour the cheesecake mixture onto your base and smooth until level. Place in the oven and bake for 40–50 minutes, or until the mixture starts to come away from the sides of the tin.

- Remove from the oven and leave to cool before placing in the fridge for 2 hours.

- Serve with some fresh raspberries or blueberries.

43g fat, 4g net carbohydrates, 2.4g fibre, 12.5g protein per serving

BLUEBERRY CLAFOUTIS

This takes minutes to prepare and is so lovely when you fancy a dessert. I serve with a dollop of Greek yoghurt or some thick cream while it is still warm. You can replace the blueberries with any other berry or cherries. You can use frozen fruit as long as the fruits aren't too wet.

Serves 8

butter for greasing
100g fresh blueberries
75g xylitol or erythritol blend (or stevia to taste)
4 eggs, beaten
zest of 1 lemon
125ml milk
200ml single or double cream
1 tsp sugar-free vanilla paste (optional)
80g plain flour

- Preheat the oven to 180°C/gas mark 4.
- Grease a flan dish (approx. 20cm) well with butter.
- Place the blueberries in the flan dish.
- Combine all the remaining ingredients together and beat well.
- Pour over the blueberries before placing into the oven.
- Bake for 30 minutes or until firm and golden.

9.1g fat, 10.3g net carbohydrates, 0.7g fibre, 5.9g protein per serving

For low carb/grain free, swap the plain flour for almond flour. 3.6g carbohydrates, 1.6g fibre.

STRAWBERRIES & CREAM POTS

So comforting! You can of course use any berries with this, but there is something lovely about strawberries with a creamy pudding!

Serves 4

2 tsp powdered gelatine (you can use sheets if you prefer)
300ml double cream
1 tsp sugar-free vanilla extract
3 tbsp xylitol or erythritol blend (or stevia to taste)
120g strawberries, sliced
300ml buttermilk

- Sprinkle the gelatine powder over 2 tbsp of water and leave to one side.

- Place the double cream, vanilla extract and sweetener in a saucepan and gently heat.

- Once it is just below a simmer, remove from the heat and stir in the gelatine until it has dissolved – I use a whisk for this.

- Leave to cool while you place strawberry slices in your ramekins – enough to cover the base of each dish.

- Once your cream mixture has cooled a little, stir in the buttermilk.

- Pour into your ramekins and place in the fridge until set – this will take 4–6 hours depending on your gelatine.

- Decorate with more strawberries before serving.

43g fat, 7.5g net carbohydrates, 1.1g fibre, 10.3g protein per serving

CHOCOLATE HAZELNUT MOUSSE

Really simple mousse that tastes impressive. If you have already made my chocolate hazelnut spread (see *The Pantry* chapter), you could just add a few good tablespoons of this, combined with 300ml of double cream, alternatively, grab your blender and follow the recipe below. I don't feel this needs any additional sweetener, but if you prefer a sweeter mousse, you can add xylitol, erythritol blend or stevia to taste.

Serves 6

250g hazelnuts, blanched
75g dark chocolate (85 per cent cocoa content, plus extra grated
    dark chocolate to decorate)
2 tbsp coconut oil
1 tbsp cocoa or cacao powder
1 tsp sugar-free vanilla extract (optional)
350ml double cream

- Preheat the oven to 160°C/gas mark 3.

- Spread the hazelnuts on a baking tray and roast for 8–10 minutes. When the nuts are warm it helps them to release their oils, making a much smoother spread. For ease of use, I use blanched hazelnuts but if you use ones with the skin on you will have to remove these before adding to the blender. You can do this by placing in a freezer bag and shaking/rolling until most of the skins are removed.

- Place the hazelnuts in a blender or processor. I use my Nutribullet. Blend until smooth.

- Melt the chocolate and coconut oil together in the microwave, 20 seconds at a time until melted, then add this to the blender along with the vanilla extract. Blend until smooth.

- Remove from the blender and place in a bowl. Pour on the cream and, using your mixer, beat until thoroughly combined. If it is too thick, add a little full fat milk. It will thicken in the fridge. Taste and add some xylitol, erythritol or stevia if you feel it needs it.

- Place in serving glasses. For adding pizzazz, add some grated dark chocolate to the top of each mousse.

- Place in the fridge for at least 1 hour before serving.

76g fat, 7.4g net carbohydrates, 5.1g fibre, 8.6g protein per serving

CHOCOLATE PECAN MERINGUE CAKE

Now, when I call this a cake, it really is more of a dessert, it is so deca-
dent – with an almost pavlova-like texture. It's one of those cakes you
simply have to eat with a cake fork, devouring while enjoying your own
private blissed-out moment. This recipe does not work with stevia.

Serves 8

9 eggs, separated
200g xylitol or erythritol blend
75ml hot water
375g pecan nuts
1 tbsp cocoa
1 tsp sugar-free vanilla extract

To decorate
Chocolate Ganache (see *The Bakery* chapter) and whipped cream
chocolate shavings
chopped pecan nuts

- Preheat the oven to 170°C/gas mark 3.

- Line two sponge tins with baking parchment.

- Place the egg whites in a clean bowl and whisk until very stiff.

- In another bowl, mix the egg yolks with the xylitol or erythritol and
  beat until really light and pale. This can take up to 10 minutes. Add
  the hot water as you beat.

- Using a food processor, whizz the pecan nuts until they are finely
  ground. Add them to your egg yolk mixture along with the cocoa and
  vanilla extract.

- Fold the pecan mixture into the egg whites very carefully.

- Place the mixture into the lined tins and spread carefully.

- Pop into the oven and cook for 1 hour. Do not open the oven during this time unless after 45–50 minutes you feel the cake may be cooking too quickly.

- Remove from the oven and leave to cool in the tray.

- When completely cool, very carefully sandwich together with chocolate ganache and/or whipped cream. You can also cover the top, but beware, it is a very delicate and fragile cake.

- Decorate with chocolate shavings and chopped pecans.

39g fat, 3.4g net carbohydrates, 4.3g fibre, 12.8g protein per serving

LEMON & PASSION FRUIT CUPS

This recipe really came about by accident. I was looking for a new pudding recipe and came across a lemon and passion fruit tart. I was on a grain-free regime and I didn't feel like making a nut pastry, so I decided to try without. I have since made this several times. Keep the egg whites as they are good to use for a pavlova or coconut macaroons (see *The Bakery* chapter). You can freeze the egg whites in a freezer bag if you don't want to use them immediately – just make a note of how many eggs are in the bag!

Serves 4

200ml double cream
3 eggs
5 egg yolks
50g erythritol or xylitol (or stevia to taste)
zest and juice of 2 lemons
2 passion fruits cut in half, pulp scooped out (including seeds)
1 tsp sugar-free vanilla extract

- Preheat the oven to 160°C/gas mark 3.
- Whisk the cream, eggs, egg yolks and sweetener together until creamy.
- Add the lemon zest and juice, passion fruit pulp and the vanilla extract and combine well.
- Pour into ramekins.
- Boil the kettle. Place the ramekins in a deep baking tin and pour boiling water into the tin until it comes halfway up the outside of the ramekins.
- Pop into the oven and cook for 25–30 minutes until firm.

- Remove from the oven and leave to cool. Place in the fridge until ready to serve.
- Serve with some cream and a handful of blueberries.

40g fat, 4.5g net carbohydrates, 1.5g fibre, 11g protein per serving

MOLTEN CHOCOLATE PUDDINGS

My son loves these, just out of the oven with their pool of melting chocolate in the middle, served with homemade ice-cream or cream. This recipe is for four but you can easily halve the recipe.

Serves 4

75g cocoa or cacao powder
120g ground almonds or almond flour
100g xylitol or erythritol blend
1 tsp sugar-free vanilla extract (optional)
75g butter, softened, plus extra to grease the ramekins
4 eggs

- Preheat the oven to 180°C/gas mark 4. Grease four ramekins with butter and finish with a sprinkle of cocoa.

- In a mixing bowl, combine all the ingredients together and whizz with your food mixer.

- Spoon into your ramekins and smooth the tops.

- Place in the oven and bake for 12–15 minutes.

- Remove, and run a knife around the edge of each ramekin before tipping out onto a plate. You can sprinkle with a little sugar-free icing sugar and add a couple of berries to the plate if you want a professional finish.

42g fat, 6.4g net carbohydrates, 9.7g fibre, 17.7g protein per serving

12

THE ICE-CREAM PARLOUR

For now, a sugar-free diet means the ice-cream aisle of your supermarket is a no-go area. At the time of writing, the only sugar-free ice-creams in the UK are *WheyHey* and *Oppo*. Both are sweetened with xylitol. Waitrose have started to stock a brand called *Only by Nature*, which offers no added sugar frozen yoghurt. These only contain naturally occurring sugars from the milk and added fruit, but why not make your own?

Ice-cream treats can be really easy to make, and if you use full fat cream and milk, you don't need to add much sweetener, if any at all.

You can make some of these recipes without an ice-cream maker, but for most ice-cream recipes, these machines do make life easier. Ice-cream makers range from basic machines costing around £20 right up to state-of-the-art machines that come in over £200.

For lollies – you will be best to invest in some good quality moulds. I prefer the silicon moulds but you can use whatever you prefer.

Use your leftovers – a wide range of food and drink can be transformed into a lolly or a base for an ice-cream. Make lollies from leftover smoothies, yoghurt, cream, milk, juices and even lemonade. For ice-cream, you can use bananas, avocados, cream, frozen fruit, milk and eggs.

CHOCOLATE BANANA GELATO

Serves 6

3 bananas, peeled and chopped, frozen
100g dark chocolate (at least 80 per cent cocoa content), melted
300ml double cream or full fat Greek yoghurt

- Place all the ingredients into your food processor and whizz until smooth and creamy.
- You can serve immediately as it will be nice and cold. Alternatively, place in a container and re-freeze until needed.
- Remember to remove from the freezer at least 5 minutes before serving.

38g fat, 14.6g net carbohydrates, 2.6g fibre, 3g protein per serving

Chocolate Bananums

My son's invention as he is a big fan of Magnums. Make the Chocolate Banana Gelato (above) and divide the mixture among six ice-lolly moulds. Once frozen, remove and immediately coat with melted dark chocolate. Place on baking parchment and re-freeze until needed.

BANANA STICKS

Really simple but kids love them.

Makes 2

1 banana
2 lolly sticks
melted dark chocolate, cream, nut butter or yoghurt
chopped almonds or hazelnuts (optional)

- Cut a banana in half and place a lolly stick into each piece.
- Dip or coat in melted chocolate, cream, nut butter or yoghurt. You can then sprinkle with chopped nuts if you prefer.
- Place in the freezer until frozen.

13.4g fat, 15.6g net carbohydrates, 3.6g fibre, 2.9g protein per serving

VANILLA ICE-CREAM

You need an ice-cream maker for this.

This is the base for lots of yummy ice-cream desserts. You can place the vanilla ice-cream between halves of banana, drizzle with my Chocolate Ganache (see *The Bakery* chapter) and sprinkle with chopped nuts to make a traditional banana split. Add some berries to this ice-cream before freezing to turn it into a berry ripple. Use your imagination and enjoy experimenting – who said sugar-free was restrictive!

This recipe uses just egg yolks, but don't throw away the egg whites, pop them into a freezer bag and freeze in batches of two or three, ready to whip up a pavlova or use to make the coconut macaroons (see *The Bakery* chapter). You can also use the egg whites to make an omelette.

Makes 12 large scoops

8 egg yolks
150g erythritol or xylitol
500ml full fat milk
500ml double or clotted cream
2 vanilla pods

- In a bowl, beat the egg yolks and sweetener together until pale and fluffy.

- Place the milk and the cream in a saucepan and gently heat on a medium heat. Add the vanilla seeds (carefully cut the pods in half lengthways and, using the tip of your knife, score down the inside of the vanilla pods to extract the seeds). I also place the empty pods into the cream mixture as it all helps to create the lovely vanilla flavour.

- Carefully add a small amount of the hot cream to the egg yolks and beat gently – do it carefully, a very small amount at a time, as you don't want the eggs to cook.

- Gradually and very carefully add all the cream and continue to whisk.

- Pour the mixture back into the pan and heat on a low heat, stirring all the time until it starts to thicken. Be careful you don't burn the base.

- Once it has started to thicken, remove from the heat and pass through a sieve into a bowl.

- Cover with cling film, and push this down into the custard as this helps to prevent a skin forming.

- Once cooled, pour the custard into your ice-cream maker. I have tried to make this without an ice-cream maker but it becomes hard and icy.

- If not serving immediately, transfer to a container and store in the freezer.

29g fat, 2.5g net carbohydrates, 0g fibre, 4g protein per scoop

RASPBERRY SORBET

You need an ice-cream maker for this.

This is traditionally made with sugar syrup, so I have substituted xylitol, erythritol blend or stevia. Xylitol or erythritol will be preferred if, like me, you don't like the aftertaste of too much stevia.

Serves 6

200ml water
100g xylitol or erythritol blend (or stevia to taste)
400g raspberries

- In a saucepan add the water and the xylitol, erythritol or stevia – add a little at a time and taste the water once dissolved to control the sweetness.
- Simmer gently until the sweetener has dissolved and the liquid starts to thicken slightly. Remove and allow to cool completely.
- Whizz your raspberries in a food processor, then push the purée through a sieve.
- When the syrup is cool, blend with the raspberries.
- Pour into the ice-cream maker and follow manufacturer's instructions for sorbet.
- Serve with a selection of berries.

0.2g fat, 3.2g net carbohydrates, 4.7g fibre, 0.8g protein per serving

MANGO, BANANA & RASPBERRY GELATO

Bananas and mangoes are a great base as they create a really smooth and creamy ice-cream. You can buy these ingredients already frozen, and I freeze bananas once they start to go brown, as my fussy boys won't eat them once they have the slightest brown mark on them!

Serves 10

2 mangoes, peeled and chopped, frozen
2 bananas, peeled and chopped, frozen
200g raspberries, frozen
500ml double cream or full fat Greek yoghurt

- Place all the ingredients into your food processor and whizz until smooth and creamy.

- As the fruit is frozen before you whizz, you can serve immediately as it will be nice and cold. Alternatively, place in a container and re-freeze until needed.

- Remember to remove from the freezer at least 5 minutes before serving as this ice-cream won't be the soft scoop type.

29g fat, 12.1g net carbohydrates, 3g fibre, 1.7g protein per serving

CHOCOLATE MAGIC SAUCE

This is a really simple version of the magic ice-cream sauce that goes hard once it settles onto the ice-cream.

Serves 4

100g dark chocolate (at least 80 per cent cocoa content)
3 tbsp coconut oil

- Place the chocolate and oil in a bowl and microwave until melted. Alternatively, melt in a bain-marie (place the bowl over a saucepan of simmering water — but don't let the water touch the base of the bowl).
- Combine well. Use this mixture over your favourite ice-cream.

318 kcal, 32.5g fat, 2g carbohydrates 1.5g fibre, 3.5g protein per serving

13

THE BAKERY

I LOVE baking. There is something wonderfully homely and comforting about the smell of cakes baking in the oven, and for me, the whole process of baking is a massive stress-buster. Whatever life throws at me, baking a cake, while listening to some good music, never fails to make me smile.

Even though we are following a sugar-free lifestyle, there is no reason why we can't still indulge in a delicious cake, biscuit or treat. The key is to choose the right ingredients, and MODERATION! Just because a cake is sugar-free, does not give you the green light to eat more than you normally would. In fact, you will find that your sweet tooth will diminish and a small piece of cake, handful of berries or piece of dark chocolate is all you'll need.

Your favourite recipes

I am not going to recreate all the family favourites here – so a word of advice. If you are not worried about grains or low carb and want to create your favourite recipe making it sugar-free, all you have to do is swap sugar for xylitol or an erythritol blend – however, I would advise you to use up to 40 per cent less than the recipe suggests in order to curb your sweet craving, and this can be reduced further as you progress on your sugar-free journey.

Reduce your sweet palate

I have worked with over 35 schools, reducing sugar intake by 40 per cent in cakes and desserts without anyone noticing any changes. You really don't need things to be as sweet. Start gradually and reduce, allowing you and your family to get used to less sweet foods, therefore reducing sweet cravings.

Sweeteners

Xylitol – Please read the opening chapters regarding xylitol. This is a really good sugar alternative, which can be used as a direct replacement for sugar, so is perfect for all your favourite recipes. Remember xylitol is very toxic to dogs.

Erythritol blends – In the UK, I use Sukrin blends or Natvia. Both are available in white sugar and icing sugar forms. Sukrin also does a lovely brown sugar alternative, called Sukrin Gold. Erythritol is not as sweet as xylitol, so producers tend to add a touch of stevia to the blend. Use as a direct replacement for sugar in your favourite recipes.

Stevia – Please read the opening chapters regarding stevia. It is a very sweet product, does not raise blood sugar and is fructose free. However, in baking, stevia can be much more problematic than xylitol or erythritol as you have to be careful how much you use – we are talking tiny amounts or you are in danger of your bakes leaving a lingering aftertaste. I have discovered liquid stevia gives less aftertaste but it does depend on the brand. I also think people's sensitivity to the taste varies, so find what works for you. *It is for this reason you will find all the recipes state the quantities for xylitol and erythritol but not for stevia as it is very much down to personal taste and the brand of stevia you use.*

Flours

Remember that flours are carbohydrates and the aim is to keep the carbs as low as possible. You can slow the digestion of carbs down by opting for wholegrain choices, spelt or buckwheat. If you opt for white flour, these will digest faster and raise your blood sugar quicker. You will also find you will be perpetuating a sugar craving, despite using a sugar-free sweetener, which is why it is best to opt for a more complex carb flour. In the recipes I recommend wholemeal, spelt or buckwheat. For these you will need to add baking powder in order to make them rise.

For low carb/grain free, you can swap the flour for almond flour or another nut flour – a combination of hazelnut flour and ground almonds works really well in cakes. I like to use either all almond flour or a 60/40 combination of almond and hazelnut. Some people find a combination of coconut flour and almond flour to be the best with a ratio of 3 parts almond flour to 1 part coconut flour, which also works really well.

You can grind your own nuts to make your own nut flours, which is by far the healthiest option. I use my Nutribullet to do this. Store ground nuts in the freezer to prevent them going rancid.

Coconut flour – If swapping to coconut flour, remember to adjust the liquid as coconut flour absorbs almost ten times its volume so if you are not careful you could have a very dry cake! I have found I have best results when baking with coconut flour. if I use 1 egg and 2 tablespoons of liquid (milk, water, buttermilk or Greek yoghurt) per 30g of coconut flour. As coconut flour is so absorbent you will need to use less coconut flour in recipes, roughly half. It does take some getting used to.

ALWAYS sieve the coconut flour before using as it can really clump up in the packaging.

The texture is always different with coconut flour, grainier and drier, but you can make quite good cakes – it just takes a little practice.

Almond flour and ground almonds – Almond flour is much finer and in cakes does give superior results, but I use ground almonds a lot and things still work out well. Almond flour is far more expensive than ground almonds. The best brand I have found in the UK is from Sukrin.

Cooking times with nut flours – Cooking times may vary when using nut flours as the mixture is a different consistency. Use my timings as a guide and check every 5 minutes after this time if they are not cooked.

Please note that when using nut flours, your bakes may be very crumbly until they are completely cold. This is particularly the case with cookies, which harden as they cool, so try not to move them too much until they are completely cold.

Cake fillings and toppings

There are some products on the market to make your own icing, such as Natvia icing mix and a nice Sukrin blend. Both work well and are a great substitute for icing sugar. I will leave that to you to experiment with, meanwhile, here are some sugar-free toppings I love, but remember, these may have a more limited shelf-life, or have to be kept in the fridge – to be honest, they never last long enough to go bad in our house!

You can of course use fresh cream and maybe add a few berries to a lovely sponge.

WARM CHOCOLATE BROWNIES

A moist chocolate brownie that kids love. When cooking brownies, always remove from the oven when they seem a bit undercooked and gooey in the middle – this will give them a nice moist texture. Cook too long and they become a bit dry and dense. See overleaf for low carb/grain-free options.

Serves 9

100g butter
80g erythritol blend or xylitol (or stevia to taste)
2 eggs
2 tbsp Greek yoghurt
1 tsp sugar-free vanilla extract (optional)
150g wholemeal, spelt or buckwheat flour
1 heaped tsp baking powder
½ tsp good quality instant coffee
1 heaped tbsp cocoa or cacao powder
100g dark chocolate (at least 80 per cent cocoa content)

- Preheat the oven to 190°C/gas mark 5.

- Place the butter and sweetener in a bowl and whisk until light and fluffy.

- Add the eggs, yoghurt and vanilla extract before adding the sifted flour and baking powder. Mix the coffee and cocoa powder with 3 tablespoons of hot water before adding this too.

- Melt the dark chocolate in the microwave (gently for 30 seconds or until melted) or melt in a bain-marie (a bowl over a small saucepan of simmering water – don't let the water touch the bottom of the bowl), and stir into the batter.

- Place the batter in a lined, greased baking tray – I use a brownie tray, which is approximately 16cm square.

- Place in the oven and cook for 20 minutes – you want it to be a little bit gooey in the middle.

- Serve warm with a handful of raspberries.

17.2g fat, 14.2g net carbohydrates, 3.7g fibre, 5.4g protein per serving

For low carb/grain free swap the flour for almond flour or ground almonds. If you prefer to use coconut flour, use 100g and add another 2 eggs and 2 tbsp of milk. Using almond flour, 4.7g carbohydrates, 4.1g fibre.

CHOCOLATE ROULADE

This is a rich dessert-style roulade but the sponge, which is fatless, is light and fluffy. If you are not used to dark chocolate, you may find this a little bit bitter as it has a very rich cocoa flavour. This recipe can be used to make a great Yule log.

Makes 8 slices

6 eggs, separated
100g erythritol blend or xylitol
1 tsp sugar-free vanilla extract
50g cocoa or cacao powder
250ml double cream
100g fresh raspberries

- Preheat the oven to 180°C/gas mark 4.
- Line a tin with baking parchment making sure the paper hangs a little over the edge of the tin as you will need to hold on to this later – I use a Swiss roll tin (39 x 24 x 2cm).
- Place the egg whites in a clean bowl and beat until they form soft peaks.
- In another bowl, whisk the egg yolks with the sweetener and vanilla until it becomes thick and doubles its size. It is important to spend some time whisking this well until it has a mousse-like texture. Sift in the cocoa and beat again.
- Take 1 tablespoon of the egg whites and add to the cocoa mixture. This helps loosen the mix. Add the remaining egg whites and very carefully fold in until combined. Don't over-mix as you will take the air out.
- Pour the mixture into the prepared tin and place in the oven for 20 minutes until firm in the centre.

- Remove from the oven and lift the cake off the tray holding on to the baking parchment. Do not remove the parchment. Place on the worktop and carefully start rolling from one end until you have a roll. Leave to cool.

- While the cake is cooling, whip the cream, then fold in the raspberries – you want some raspberries crushed and some whole.

- Carefully unroll the sponge. Don't press down on it or it may split. Carefully add the cream filling before re-rolling. Place on a plate, ready to serve.

- Due to the filling, this will have to be refrigerated; however, if you opt for a different filling for a few days it should keep in an airtight container. You can also freeze this sponge.

22g fat, 1.7g net carbohydrates, 1.6g fibre, 6.7g protein per slice

SUGAR-FREE BERRY MUFFINS

I love berries. These muffins are far better if you use fresh berries rather than frozen, as frozen tend to be a bit too wet.

Makes 12

150g butter
100g erythritol blend or xylitol (or stevia to taste)
3 eggs, beaten
175g wholemeal self-raising, spelt or buckwheat flour
1 tsp baking powder
80g mixed berries (blueberries, redcurrants, raspberries etc.)

- Preheat the oven to 180°C/gas mark 4.
- Beat the butter and sweetener together until light and fluffy.
- Gradually add the eggs with a tablespoon of flour then fold in the sifted flour and baking powder.
- Add the mixed berries and fold in carefully.
- Spoon into muffin cases.
- Bake on the middle shelf of the oven for 20 minutes, or until firm and golden.

11.9g fat, 9.9g net carbohydrates, 1.6g fibre, 3.6g protein per muffin

For grain free, swap the grain flour for 125g almond flour and 30g coconut flour or hazelnut flour. (You can also use 175g almond flour if you prefer. If you use all coconut flour, you only need 120g and add another 2 eggs and 3 tbsp of milk.) 2.2g carbohydrates, 3.1g fibre.

NUTTY CHOCOLATE CHIP COOKIES

You can buy low-sugar dark chocolate chips but they are not easy to find. I have some 85 per cent cocoa and some 95 per cent. I did find some sugar-free ones but they were full of artificial sweeteners. If you don't have the chocolate chips, you can bash up a bar of dark chocolate.

Makes 15

100g butter
70g erythritol blend or xylitol (or stevia to taste)
1 egg, beaten
½ tsp baking powder
200g plain wholemeal, spelt or buckwheat flour
50g hazelnuts, roughly chopped
75g extra dark chocolate chips

- Preheat the oven to 180°C/gas mark 4.
- Beat the butter and sweetener together until light and fluffy.
- Add the egg before folding in all the remaining ingredients.
- Line your baking trays with greaseproof paper. Place large spoonfuls of the dough onto the trays. Using the back of a spoon, press down gently onto each mound to form a cookie shape.
- Place in the oven and bake for 15–18 minutes until golden. Leave on a cooling rack until cool, before storing in an airtight container.

10.8g fat, 10g net carbohydrates, 2.2g fibre, 3g protein per cookie

For low carb, swap the plain flour for almond flour. 2.4g carbohydrates, 2.5g fibre.

GRAIN-FREE DARK CHOCOLATE & WALNUT CAKE

This is a really rich, dark chocolate cake, peppered with a sprinkle of walnuts to add a little texture. It is delicious warm with some extra thick cream and a handful of berries, or have it cold with your cuppa.

Serves 10

180g butter
100g xylitol or erythritol blend
4 eggs, beaten
140g ground almonds
1 heaped tsp baking powder
40g cocoa or cacao powder
40g walnuts, chopped
40g extra dark chocolate chips (95 per cent cocoa)

- Preheat the oven to 160°C/gas mark 3. Line a 22cm spring-form cake tin – I use cake liners as they are so easy.
- Place the butter and the sweetener in your mixer and beat until light and fluffy.
- Add all the remaining ingredients and combine well. It will be quite a thick batter.
- Dollop into the lined cake tin.
- Place in the oven and bake for 30–40 minutes until firm.
- Remove from the oven and place on a cooling rack (or eat while still warm). Once cooled, store in an airtight container.

31g fat, 3.2g net carbohydrates, 3.9g fibre, 7.9g protein per serving

COCONUT MACAROON BISCUITS

These are slightly different to the coconut macaroons that are piled high with fluffy coconut. These are more like a biscuit and are great on their own or topped with some melted dark chocolate. This recipe is not good with stevia, so use erythritol blend or xylitol.

Makes 12

4 egg whites
120g erythritol blend or xylitol
300g unsweetened desiccated coconut

- Preheat the oven to 160°C/gas mark 3. Line a baking tray with baking parchment.

- Whisk the egg whites until light and fluffy.

- Blend in the sweetener and coconut and combine gently.

- Place a spoonful of the mixture onto the parchment. Using the back of a dessertspoon, press down on the mixture and spread gently to form a flatter circle. Continue until you use all the mixture.

- Place in the oven and cook for 10 minutes or until golden. Watch them carefully as you do not want them to burn.

- Remove from the oven and place on a cooling rack. Once cooled, store in an airtight tin.

15.6g fat, 1.6g net carbohydrates, 5.3g fibre, 2.6g protein per biscuit

CHOCOLATE TORTE

This is seriously good and would pass muster at a dinner party. It is lush with a dollop of cream and some raspberries – mind you, for me, everything is lovely with cream and raspberries!

Serves 8

275g dark chocolate (at least 85 per cent cocoa)
5 eggs, separated
150g erythritol blend or xylitol (or stevia to taste)
140g almond flour or ground almonds

- Oil and line a 20cm round tin. Preheat the oven to 180°C/gas mark 4.

- Melt the dark chocolate in a bain-marie (a bowl over a small saucepan of simmering water – don't let the water touch the bottom of the bowl) or very carefully in a microwave (this takes seconds).

- In a clean bowl, whisk the egg whites until they form soft peaks.

- In another bowl, whisk the egg yolks with the sweetener until light and fluffy.

- Carefully fold half the egg whites into the egg yolk mixture, gently add the chocolate, then the rest of the egg whites – being careful not to remove all the air. Finally, fold in the almonds.

- Pour this mixture into the tin before placing in the oven. Bake for 30 minutes. Turn off the oven and keep in for another 10 minutes.

- The torte will be cracked on top but this is as it should be. You can finish with a sprinkle of cocoa.

31g fat, 9.3g net carbohydrates, 6.2g fibre, 11.3g protein per serving

BUTTERMILK SCONES

This is a recipe my mum and I use again and again when we are teaching children cookery. The reason? Unlike most other scone recipes, this mix can be really abused and over-handled yet still turns out perfect time after time. This is our traditional recipe, but swapping sugar for erythritol blend or xylitol. Stevia can be used but you will have to add a very small amount to taste, and be careful of the aftertaste.

Makes 6

100ml buttermilk
1 egg, beaten
75g chilled butter, cut into small pieces
250g wholemeal self-raising, spelt or buckwheat flour
1 tsp baking powder
75g erythritol blend or xylitol
a little milk or beaten egg to brush the tops

- Preheat the oven to 200°C/gas mark 6.
- Combine the buttermilk and egg and leave to one side.
- In a bowl, rub the butter into the flour and baking powder until it resembles breadcrumbs.
- Add the erythritol blend or xylitol and combine well.
- Pour on the buttermilk mixture and stir with a wooden spoon. Once it starts to form a dough, you can use your hands to bring the dough together.
- Place onto a lightly floured board and press down to around 5cm thick.
- Using a cutter, cut out six scones.
- Brush with milk or beaten egg before placing in the oven.

- Cook for 12–15 minutes until golden.

- Place on a cooling tray to cool slightly before serving with clotted cream and sugar-free chia raspberry jam (see *The Pantry* chapter).

12.1g fat, 28g net carbohydrates, 4.2g fibre, 6.7g protein per scone

For low carb/grain free you can swap the flour for almond flour – it does change the texture but is still very tasty. If you use coconut flour, only use 200g, and add 2 more eggs and double the buttermilk. Nutritional values using almond flour are 3.9g carbohydrates, 5.4g fibre.

BAKEWELL TART

A family favourite. You can top this with flaked almonds as described below or, if you prefer, some sugar-free icing. This can be made with traditional pastry or a grain-free pastry. Use the sugar-free raspberry jam found in *The Pantry* chapter.

Serves 8

Pastry
175g wholemeal, buckwheat or spelt flour
75g chilled butter, cut into small pieces

Batter
125g butter, softened
100g erythritol blend or xylitol (or stevia to taste)
125g almond flour or ground almonds
1 egg, beaten
1 tsp almond essence
1–2 tbsp sugar-free raspberry jam or 50g crushed fresh raspberries
30g flaked almonds

- Preheat the oven to 180°C/gas mark 4.
- To make the pastry, rub the butter into the flour until it resembles breadcrumbs.
- Add 2–3 tablespoons of very cold water and form into a dough. Leave to chill for 10 minutes in the fridge while you make the batter.
- Place the butter and erythritol blend or xylitol into a bowl and beat until light and fluffy.
- Add the almonds, egg and almond essence and beat well until combined evenly.

- Roll out the pastry and line a 20cm tin.

- Place the jam or raspberries onto the pastry and spread in a thin layer. Don't be tempted to add too much jam as it will bubble up and spill.

- Pour on the cake batter and smooth the top. Finish with a sprinkle of flaked almonds.

- Place in the oven and cook for 30–40 minutes until golden on top and the sponge springs back when touched.

- Remove from the oven and leave to cool before slicing. Store in an airtight container.

32g fat, 15.6g net carbohydrates, 5.1g fibre, 7.8g protein per serving

For low carb/grain free, rub 40g butter into 300g ground almonds and 75g ground hazelnuts. Add 2 eggs. Roll out between two sheets of baking parchment before lining your tin. 4.7g carbohydrates, 8.4g fibre.

LEMON & BLUEBERRY POLENTA CAKE

This is a really moist cake. I sometimes make double the quantity and fill two sandwich tins to make a lemon sponge, filling the centre with my sugar-free lemon curd (see *The Pantry* chapter).

Serves 8

175g butter
120g erythritol blend or xylitol (or stevia to taste)
3 eggs
zest and juice of 3 lemons
250g fine polenta
3 tsp baking powder
40g blueberries

- Preheat the oven to 180°C/gas mark 4. Grease and line a 22cm round cake tin.

- Beat the butter and sweetener together until light and fluffy. Add the eggs and beat well.

- Add the lemon zest juice and the polenta. Stir in the baking powder. Carefully fold in the blueberries.

- Pour the cake mixture into your lined tin and bake for 30 minutes or until a skewer inserted into the centre of the cake comes out clean.

- Turn out onto a cooling rack and allow to cool before slicing – if you can, it is delicious hot!

21g fat, 23g net carbohydrates, 2.5g fibre, 5.4g protein per serving

For low carb/grain free, this cake works brilliantly with almond flour. 3.1g carbohydrates, 4.2g fibre.

LOW-CARB SUPER-MOIST LEMON DRIZZLE CAKE

Lemon drizzle was one of my dad's favourite cakes. This is a low-carb/grain-free version which is super-moist, even a few days after it has been cooked. You can top this with the remaining lemon juice when it is first out of the oven, or wait until cool and spread the slices with sugar-free lemon curd (see *The Pantry* chapter). This is also lovely with some blueberries mixed into the batter before cooking.

Makes 10 slices

100g butter
100g full fat cream cheese
75g erythritol blend or xylitol
90g almond flour or ground almonds
40g coconut flour
1 tsp baking power
zest of 2–3 lemons (squeeze the juice to drizzle over the hot cake)
5 eggs

- Preheat the oven to 170°C/gas mark 3. Line a 900g, loaf tin with baking parchment – or use a loaf tin liner.

- Beat the butter, cream cheese and sweetener together until pale and creamy.

- Add all the remaining ingredients and combine well.

- Pour into the lined loaf tin.

- Place into the oven and bake for 45–50 minutes. The cake should be golden on top, but because it is made with grain-free flour it will still have a little softness to it. To check that it is cooked, insert a knife or skewer into the centre of the cake; it should come out clean.

- Spoon some of the lemon juice over the cake while it is still hot.

- Leave to cool completely – any cake made with almond or coconut flour needs to cool or it can be very crumbly.
- Once cooled, store in an airtight container.

18.9g fat, 1.9g net carbohydrates, 2.9g fibre, 6.8g protein per slice

CHESTNUT & FLAX SEED BREAD
(SUGAR/GRAIN/YEAST FREE)

This bread is suitable for a low carb diet. I have tried lots of other low carb bread recipes (including many that have come out purple thanks to psyllium husk) but this one is always good and very filling.

This bread contains 5g of omega-3 and is high in vitamin B2, magnesium and phosphorus.

Makes 1lb loaf (approx. 8 thick slices)

50g butter or 1 tbsp coconut oil

4 eggs

3 tbsp water

120g ground flax seeds

60g almond flour (or use coconut flour or chestnut flour)

1 tsp baking powder

1 tsp cream of tartar

30g mixed seeds

- Preheat the oven to 180°C/gas mark 4.
- Beat the butter until soft – if using coconut oil, simply melt and place in your bowl. Add the eggs and water and beat well.
- Mix in all the remaining ingredients, combining well.
- Place in a 500g loaf tin and bake for 30–40 minutes until golden and firm.
- Cool on a cooling rack before slicing.

21g fat, 1.5g net carbohydrates, 5.4g fibre, 9.4g protein per serving

CHOCOLATE GANACHE

This is really easy to make, but watch the sugar content of your chocolate. Use as high a cocoa content as you can.

200g dark chocolate (90–95 per cent coca)
250ml cream

- Grate the dark chocolate and place to one side.
- Put the cream into a saucepan and pop onto a medium heat. Heat gently – don't let it boil.
- Once it has come up to temperature, remove from the heat.
- Add the grated chocolate and stir well until it has melted; it will start to thicken and become glossy.
- Cool before using on a cake or dessert.

RICH CHOCOLATE FAUX BUTTERCREAM

It takes minutes to make this chocolate buttercream style cake topping. You can pipe it into lovely cupcake swirls, perfect for cake decorating.

If you find sugar-free cacao or cocoa too bitter, you could prepare this with melted dark chocolate or sugar-free chocolate.

1 large, ripe avocado, mashed
1 tbsp coconut oil, melted
1–2 tbsp cocoa or cacao (depending on taste)
rice malt syrup (or liquid stevia) to taste
1–3 tbsp full fat milk

- Place the mashed avocado in a bowl and add the melted coconut oil and cocoa and combine well.

- Add a little rice malt syrup or liquid stevia to taste (taste as you go).

- Add a little milk until you get the consistency you require, depending on whether you are piping or spreading onto a cake.

- **NB:** You can flavour this by adding hazelnuts, mint essence or orange essence.

LEMON CREAM FILLING

This is one of my favourites, but it does have to be stored in the fridge. I use this with a little sugar-free lemon curd to fill a lemon sponge or on lemon butterfly cupcakes. It is also lovely with some crushed raspberries.

120g cream cheese
3 tbsp thick cream or Greek yoghurt
zest of 1 large lemon

- Beat the cream cheese, cream and lemon zest together until well combined.
- If you want a thinner mixture, add a little milk or lemon juice until you get the required consistency.

RASPBERRY CREAM FILLING

This is a lovely filling between the layers of a Victoria sponge or rich dark chocolate cake.

120g cream cheese
3 tbsp thick cream or Greek yoghurt
80g fresh or frozen raspberries

- Beat the cream cheese and cream together until well combined.
- If you are using frozen raspberries, drain off any liquid (reserving the liquid in a jug in case you need it later). Mix with the cream mixture.
- If you want a thinner mixture, add a little of the drained raspberry juice or milk until you get the required consistency.

EASY CREAMED FROSTING

A very easy base for any flavour frosting.

200g Greek yoghurt
200g cream cheese
1–2 tsp sugar-free vanilla extract

- Beat the ingredients together until you have a smooth, creamy consistency.
- Add any flavouring you wish (cocoa, lemon, raspberry, coffee) and beat well.

14

THE TUCK SHOP

O NE of the things we think when we embark on a sugar-free diet is that we will never be having anything sweet again, particularly chocolates or sweeties. But this chapter is full of my adaptations on our favourite sweets and savoury nibbles.

Here I will demonstrate that you can have your sweets and treats when you follow a sugar-free lifestyle, but it is also important to emphasise that I don't want you to binge on these! There is a risk if you have too many sweet foods that you may start craving sugary snacks and we really don't want to encourage that.

Sweetness does vary depending on personal taste so my suggestions are guides only. As you get used to a sugar-free lifestyle, you will find you rely less and less on the natural sweeteners.

As mentioned in the opening chapters, stevia can leave a lingering aftertaste. I use liquid stevia, but the aftertaste does vary depending on the brand and your own personal susceptibility. You can opt for flavoured stevia liquid, which can be quite helpful for the recipes in this chapter. If in doubt, opt for xylitol or erythritol blend.

Chocolate tips

- You will need to opt for dark chocolate for all these recipes, ideally with as much cocoa content as you can find. Check the sugar content as it does vary between brands. You can also buy sugar-free chocolate sweetened with stevia or xylitol. I am for at least 95 per cent (Lindt do a nice one) but my favourite is 100 per cent from www.chococo.co.uk.

- I melt my chocolate in a microwave, using the Lakeland Silicon melting pot, but you can use a bain-marie method if you prefer. I microwave the chocolate in 30-second intervals, making sure it does not burn. If you prefer, you can melt your chocolate in a bain-marie (a bowl over a small saucepan of simmering water – don't let the water touch the bottom of the bowl).

- I love using silicon chocolate moulds. You can pick these up quite cheaply and they do give your chocolates a professional look. I use a paint brush to coat the moulds, refrigerating or freezing between each coating.

- Sweetness does vary depending on personal taste so my suggestions are guides only. As you get used to a sugar-free lifestyle, you will find you rely less and less on the natural sweeteners.

- As mentioned in the opening chapters, stevia can leave a lingering aftertaste. I use liquid stevia, but the aftertaste does vary depending on the brand and your own personal susceptibility. You can opt for flavoured stevia liquid, which can be quite helpful for the recipes in this chapter. If in doubt, opt for xylitol or erythritol blend.

Remember you will need less sugar and opt for stronger dark chocolate as your palate changes. Try not to be too reliant on adding these to your diet, they are treats and not everyday foods.

Savoury treats

Once we are established on a sugar-free diet, we also try hard to avoid anything processed as it may contain added sugars. This chapter includes some savoury nibbles you may enjoy in place of the traditional crisps and savoury snacks.

CHOCOLATE MINT BITES

You can make these in a baking tray and cut into squares before dipping into chocolate or if you want to be a bit fancy, you can use a silicon chocolate mould (which I prefer). Coat the moulds with dark chocolate before adding the filling, then cover again with chocolate. Freeze between each stage to speed up the process.

Makes 18–20

200g dark chocolate (at least 85 per cent cocoa)
100g coconut oil, melted
4 tbsp extra thick cream
1 tsp peppermint extract
1–3 drops of liquid stevia or 2–3 tsp xylitol (optional)

- Melt the chocolate. I do this in the microwave, checking every 30 seconds until melted.

- If you are making in a baking tray, line this with greaseproof paper (I use a 22cm square tin). Pour half the chocolate into your tray and spread to form an even layer. Place in the fridge or freezer until set.

- Alternatively, you can line your silicon chocolate moulds with the melted chocolate, then place in the fridge or freezer until set.

- Mix the melted coconut oil with the extra thick cream and peppermint extract. It will curdle at first but keep stirring with a small hand whisk or fork. It will start to thicken as it cools. If you like a sweet taste, you could add some stevia or a sprinkle of xylitol to taste.

- Pour the mint mixture onto the set chocolate base (or fill the chocolate moulds) and return to the fridge or freezer to set.

- When set, cover with the remaining dark chocolate and re-freeze/ refrigerate until needed.

- If using the tray method, remove from the tray and cut into small squares. Store in an airtight container in the fridge.

12.2g fat, 2.7g net carbohydrates, 1.3g fibre, 1.1g protein per serving

SUGAR-FREE FAUX FERRERO ROCHER

I must confess that I had very little to do with this recipe. My son decided to make my sugar-free chocolate spread. I left him to it and only intervened when he shouted that the mixture was too thick. He had blended everything together instead of blending the hazelnuts first, so we ended up with a thick chocolate mixture with a combination of whole and blended hazelnuts. It tasted amazing and we soon realised it was exactly like Ferrero Rocher. We then abandoned the idea of chocolate spread, made these into balls and then coated them with chocolate. How wonderful!

I do not use sweetener in this but feel free to add a small amount if you feel it needs it.

Makes 20

200g hazelnuts, blanched (plus 20 hazelnuts for centres)
75g dark chocolate
2 tbsp coconut oil
1 tbsp cocoa or cacao powder
1 tsp sugar-free vanilla extract (optional)

To coat
75g dark chocolate
2 tbsp coconut oil
30g hazelnuts, chopped

- Preheat the oven to 160°C/gas mark 3. Spread the hazelnuts on a baking tray and roast for 8–10 minutes (heating them will release the oils, which makes it easier to blend them). For ease of use, I use blanched hazelnuts but if you use ones with the skin on you will have to remove the skin before adding to the blender. You can do this after they have been heated by placing them in a freezer bag and shaking/ rolling to remove most of the skins.

- While the hazelnuts are in the oven, melt the chocolate and coconut oil together.

- Place all the ingredients (apart from the 20 extra hazelnuts) into a blender or processor. I use my Nutribullet. Blend until smooth.

- Scrape out into a bowl and form into 20 balls – if you want a hazelnut centre, pop a hazelnut into each ball before placing on a sheet of greaseproof paper.

- Refrigerate for 20 minutes.

- To coat the balls, melt the chocolate and coconut oil together, combine well. Dip the balls into the chocolate (I place each ball on the end of a fork to dip) or pour the chocolate over the balls – whatever you find easier. Sprinkle with some chopped hazelnuts. Refrigerate again until set.

16.7g fat, 2.6g net carbohydrates, 1.8g fibre, 2.4g protein per serving

CHOCOLATE ORANGE CREAMS

I make these in silicon chocolate moulds as they look really lovely. The orange flavour depends on the type of flavouring you use. I have tried several and they vary so the key is to taste as you make it, as too much can be too artificial. For adults only, why not add some Cointreau to the mixture?

Makes 20

200g dark chocolate
100g coconut oil
4 tbsp thick cream
orange flavouring (to taste)
1–3 drops of stevia liquid (optional) or sweetener of your choice
orange food colouring (optional)

- Melt half the chocolate in the microwave or bain-marie.
- Coat the silicon moulds with the chocolate. I use a brush to do this.
- Place in the fridge or freezer to set. Once set, you may wish to line again if you want a nice thick chocolate.
- When ready, melt the coconut oil. Add the cream. This will curdle but use a fork or a whisk and keep stirring as it will come together. As it cools it will thicken.
- Add your flavouring, sweetener (if needed), and optional colouring. If you are using Cointreau, add 1–2 tbsp to the mixture. Taste as you go to achieve the correct strength of flavour and sweetness that suits you.
- Remove the moulds from the fridge and fill with the orange mixture. Place back into the fridge for 10 minutes.
- Melt the remaining dark chocolate. Pour into the moulds to cover the orange cream before placing back into the fridge.

- Once set, turn out and pop into an airtight container. I keep these in the fridge until eaten.

12.2g fat, 2.7g net carbohydrates, 1.3g fibre, 1.1g protein per serving

Lemon creams – use lemon flavouring and yellow food colouring instead of orange for adults only, add some Limoncello to the mixture.

DARK CHOCOLATE COCONUT BARS

These are really easy to make and kids love them. They store well in the freezer so you can batch cook.

Makes 8

200g unsweetened desiccated coconut
2 tbsp coconut oil, melted
1–2 tbsp rice malt syrup or erythritol or xylitol (or stevia to taste)
4 tbsp coconut cream
150g dark chocolate (or melted raw cacao)

- Combine all the ingredients apart from the chocolate in a bowl.
- Mould the mixture into eight small sausage shapes and place on a baking tray.
- Place the tray in the freezer and leave until frozen.
- Once frozen, melt the chocolate (either in a microwave or bain-marie).
- Remove the coconut bars from the freezer and coat with the chocolate. You can either spear them onto a fork and dip them into the chocolate or coat one side at a time, turning once set. Place on a sheet of baking parchment and place in the fridge or freezer until set.
- Store these in the fridge or freezer.

35g fat, 6.5g net carbohydrates, 7.6g fibre, 3.4g protein per bar

CHOCOLATE BARK

Try to get your children used to the taste of dark chocolate as it contains less sugar than milk chocolate. You can sprinkle the chocolate with a variety of nuts, seeds or coconut flakes so feel free to adapt to suit your taste or what is in your store cupboard. You can also try some freeze-dried strawberries or raspberries.

Makes approx. 12 pieces

200g dark chocolate (at least 80 per cent cocoa)
2 tsp coconut oil
1–2 tbsp coconut flakes
1–2 tbsp goji berries
1–2 tbsp flaked almonds

- Line a baking tin with baking parchment. (I use a 20cm tin.)
- Melt the chocolate and coconut oil together using a bain-marie or the microwave.
- Pour into your lined baking tin, spreading evenly with a palette knife.
- Sprinkle on your chosen toppings, pushing them down slightly to help secure them into the chocolate.
- Place in the fridge for at least 1 hour.
- Cut into squares and store in an airtight container in the fridge.

14.9g fat, 4.9g net carbohydrates, 2.4g fibre, 2g protein per serving

NUT BUTTER FUDGE

You can use peanut butter in this if you aren't worried about the carbs, but if you want a lower carb version, you can make your own nut butter. Spread 200g blanched nuts on a baking tray and roast at 160°C/gas mark 3 for 8–10 minutes. Blend until smooth in a blender, food processor or Nutribullet. If you are using a jar of nut butter, ensure the only ingredients listed on the jar are nuts. I like Meridian brand – they offer a range of nut butters and are available in supermarkets.

Makes 12 pieces

220g coconut oil
200g nut butter
4 tbsp double cream
1 tsp sugar-free vanilla extract (optional)

- Melt the coconut oil and place with all the remaining ingredients in a blender.
- Whizz until smooth.
- Pour into a lined tin – I use a small Pyrex dish approx. 20cm square.
- Flatten before placing in the fridge to set. Leave for at least 3 hours.
- You can drizzle some dark chocolate over the top or just leave as is.
- When ready to serve, cut into chunks. Store in an airtight container and keep in the fridge.

30g fat, 1.3g net carbohydrates, 2.6g fibre, 3.5g protein per serving

COCONUT ICE

I used to eat this as a child, but I think my mum used condensed milk in her recipe. It was probably packed with sugar! This recipe is sugar-free but is well worth a try and is so easy to make. You can colour half the mixture to create the traditional pink and white coconut ice.

Makes 30 squares

400g coconut milk
150g coconut oil
100g erythritol blend or xylitol
600g unsweetened desiccated coconut

- Place the coconut milk and coconut oil in a pan and heat until melted and combined well.
- Add the sweetener and stir until dissolved.
- Remove from the heat and add the desiccated coconut, stirring well to ensure it is evenly coated in the milky mixture.
- Place in a lined baking tin (I use a tin approx. 22cm square).
- Place in the fridge for at least 3 hours to set before slicing.

22g fat, 1.6g net carbohydrates, 4.3g fibre, 1.3g protein per serving

COCONUT & ALMOND BARFI (INDIAN SWEET)

This recipe was created by Sukhy Dosanjh Lally, and she has very kindly given me permission to share this with you all. It is seriously yummy and so simple.

Makes 12

100g butter
300ml double cream
4 crushed cardamoms (with husks removed)
3 heaped tbsp ground almonds
200g unsweetened desiccated coconut

- In a pan, melt the butter and cream together with the crushed cardamoms.
- When the cream starts to warm and coat the sides of the pan (about 5 minutes on a low heat), add the ground almonds and desiccated coconut.
- Mix all the ingredients thoroughly and flatten into a grease-proof-lined tin (20cm square) and smooth the top. You can sprinkle flaked almonds or crushed pistachio nuts on top and gently press down.
- Place in the fridge for 3 hours to chill and set. Once chilled, remove and cut into diamond shapes. Place in an airtight container and store in the fridge.

33g fat, 2.1g net carbohydrates, 4.3g fibre, 2.5g protein per serving

Gelatine jellied sweets

Gelatine doesn't sound very appealing and it certainly doesn't sound like something to be encouraged, but – unless you are vegetarian – think again. Gelatine helps promote the right environment for healthy bacteria in the gut. It is also very protective of the digestive tract. It can improve joint health and strengthen hair and nails. I use grass-fed beef gelatine powder but the choice is yours. If you use gelatine sheets, place in cold water to go limp before adding to the warm liquid.

You can buy fantastic silicon moulds online (Amazon and Lakeland are my favourites) in all shapes and sizes. I love the jelly bear moulds. I also fill these with leftover smoothies and freeze. Great to serve with some berries and kids love them!

I remember quite a few years ago when my eldest son came home from school with a party bag containing a well-known brand of jellied sweets. I wanted to educate him on why I restricted these sweets. I asked him to read the ingredients and I pretended to consider how to make them. Some ingredients we recognised, such as beeswax, but others were e numbers and colourings. Looking these up was an eye opener for him and I won't disgust you with the details but let's just say you wouldn't order them on a menu! Since then he never wanted to eat those sweets!

SUGAR-FREE BERRY-JELLY BEARS

If you are using raspberries or strawberries, you may want to sieve to remove the seeds before adding to the liquid.

Makes 24

80g fresh or frozen berries of your choice
200ml water, milk or coconut water (milk makes a cloudy jelly
  bear!)
2 tbsp erythritol blend or xylitol (or a few drops of stevia liquid to
  taste)
lemon juice
4 tbsp powdered gelatine

- I use my Nutribullet to pulp the fruit (adding a little water to help blend) but you can use a blender or just mush together as thoroughly as you can until you have a smooth pulp.

- In a pan, heat the water, sweetener and lemon juice until combined and warm. Add the gelatine and stir with a whisk until combined and the water starts to look a bit glossy and smooth.

- Add the fruit purée and combine well before carefully placing in your silicon moulds. This is not as easy as it sounds so ensure you use a good jug with a nice pouring action or it could get messy. I also place my moulds onto a baking sheet before adding liquid in order to keep them nice and stable when I transport them to the fridge.

- Leave in the fridge until set.

0.01g fat, 0.2g net carbohydrates, 0.1g fibre, 2.1g protein per
  serving

FINGER-LICKING ALMONDS

These are really moreish, so you have been warned! I like to eat these when I get a craving for crisps – normally, if I am honest, when I am enjoying a little tipple!

300g whole almonds
1–2 tsp chilli powder
1 tsp garlic powder
1 tsp dried thyme
2 tsp paprika
generous sprinkle of sea salt
black pepper
1 tbsp melted coconut oil or olive oil

- Preheat the oven to 170°C/gas mark 3.
- Place all the ingredients in a bowl and combine well, ensuring all the almonds are equally covered.
- Pour onto a baking tray and bake for 8 minutes.
- Remove from oven and allow to cool.
- Store in an airtight container.

54g fat, 6.7g net carbohydrates, 15g fibre, 18.7g protein per 100g

SWEET CINNAMON NUTS

These are really nice to have on top of some natural yoghurt. They are also good with some chopped apple. They remind me of the flavours of Christmas.

300g nuts (almonds, pecans, walnuts or macadamia nuts)
2 tbsp coconut oil, melted
2 tsp ground cinnamon
1 tsp allspice
1 tsp mixed spice
2 tsp Sukrin Gold (optional)

- Preheat the oven to 150°C/gas mark 2.
- Place the nuts in a bowl, add the coconut oil, spices and Sukrin Gold.
- Combine well, ensuring the nuts are completely covered.
- Pour onto a baking tray and spread so they are in a single layer.
- You can finish with a sprinkle of cinnamon.
- Pop into the oven for 5–8 minutes – no more or they will start to burn.
- Remove from oven and allow to cool before placing in an airtight container.

55g fat, 6.7g net carbohydrates, 15.2g fibre, 18.9g protein per 100g

Crisps

Although crisps are not filled with sugar, they are refined carbohydrates and not particularly healthy – but sometimes you just want something salty and crisp to crunch. Below are a couple of recipes but you can also opt for baking bacon in the oven until extra crisp. You can also thinly slice pepperoni and bake this until ultra-crisp. Pork scratchings, beef jerky and biltong are also good alternatives and are readily available in supermarkets.

PARMESAN CRISPS

The instructions below are for the microwave, but you can make these in the oven if you're careful they don't burn.

- Using 4 tbsp of grated Parmesan, place 12 of the cheese on a sheet of greaseproof paper and spread evenly to form circles.
- Pop into the microwave and cook on high for 1–2 minutes depending on the power of your oven (start at 1 minute and then in 20-second intervals until golden – don't overcook).
- The Parmesan will melt and bubble – it is done when it has gone slightly golden.
- Remove from the microwave.
- Leave until it cools and it will set.

KALE CRISPS

These are really tasty so do try them. You can coat them with whatever spices you like, such as chilli, garlic, or even nutritional yeast flakes, which give a cheesy flavour. You can keep things simple and opt for sea salt, black pepper and paprika, but the combination below is my personal favourite.

Note: I was sent a dehydrator from Lakeland to review and I can seriously recommend them: the crisps come out beautifully dry and crisp.

Makes 1 large bowlful

200g kale
1 tbsp melted coconut oil or olive oil
sea salt
black pepper
1 tsp paprika
1 tsp garlic powder
½ tsp dried thyme
½ tsp chilli powder

- Preheat the oven to 150°C/gas mark 2.
- Wash and dry your kale, making sure it is perfectly dry. Remove any stems and thick bits, just leaving the nice leaves.
- Place in a bowl and add the oil along with your flavourings. Combine well to ensure it is all evenly coated.
- Place on a well-greased or lined baking tray and cook for 20–30 minutes. Turn off the oven but leave the kale inside to dry out more.
- Remove when cool and enjoy! Store in an airtight container.

15

THE PANTRY

This was one of my favourite chapters to put together. It contains a range of pantry essentials including spice blends and bone stock. My clients are always shocked when they discover the everyday items they thought were free from sugar, actually contain quite a substantial amount. Tomato Sauce is one item that is commented on the most (along with Nutella Chocolate Spread). I love creating my own condiments, jams, chutneys and spice blends. It is usually something I do on a Sunday afternoon, with the radio to keep me company. I collect glass jars, sterilising them in the dishwasher before filling them. The jams, curds and sauces are kept in the fridge. The spice blends lasts for months in airtight jars in my pantry.

STOCKS AND GRAVY

BONE BROTH/STOCK

This is a really healthy broth, much better for you than processed stock cubes. It is packed with minerals such as calcium, magnesium and phosphorus. It helps support the digestive tract, boosts the immune system, reduces inflammation, as well as strengthening joints, hair and nails and promoting healthy skin. Speak to your butcher as they are often happy to give away bones for you to use.

Invest in a large stock pot to make up several litres at a time and store in the fridge or freezer. I store in freezer bags as well as some large silicon ice moulds. The freezer bags can be defrosted quickly by popping the sealed bag into a bowl of water. I use the silicon moulds to pop out a few 'ice stock cubes' to add to dishes such as a chilli or spaghetti bolognaise.

Instead of a large stock pot you could use your slow cooker or a pressure cooker.

1kg bones (marrow bones, ribs, knuckles, etc.)
200ml apple cider vinegar
2 large onions, chopped into quarters
2 cloves of garlic, cut into chunks
2 carrots, cut into chunks
2–3 sticks of celery, cut into chunks

2 tsp mixed herbs

small handful of fresh parsley (or 2–3 tsp dried)

2–3 bay leaves

2 tsp peppercorns

- If using meaty bones, place in the oven and roast for 45 minutes to help release the flavours and nutrients. You can omit this step if you prefer.
- Place all the ingredients into your stock pot and cover with water.
- Simmer gently for 24–48 hours for beef bones, 12–24 hours for chicken.
- Remove any scum from the surface of the water occasionally. Just scoop it out with a spoon.
- When cooked, remove from the heat, strain and leave to cool.
- A layer of fat will form on the top once cooled. Don't discard this, save it to use as a cooking fat.
- Store in a jar, freezer bag or silicon ice moulds ready to use in your everyday savoury dishes.

For vegetarian stock, just add a variety of vegetables and herbs to taste and cook at a low simmer for 1–2 hours or 6–8 hours in a slow cooker.

SPREADS, JAMS AND CHUTNEYS

HAZELNUTTY CHOCOLATE SPREAD

It is really shameful the amount of sugar, palm oil, and skimmed milk powder in commercial chocolate spreads (the leading brand in chocolate spread is almost 60 per cent sugar). This is a really easy recipe that will satisfy any chocolate addict. It is sugar-free and sweetener free as I really don't think it needs anything else! however, if you have a very sweet tooth, you can add some erythritol, xylitol or a drop of stevia liquid to taste – though remember, you need to start adjusting your palate to less sweet options and this is a fantastic start!

Makes 1 jar (approx. 500g)

350g hazelnuts, blanched
100g sugar-free dark chocolate
2 tbsp coconut oil
1 tbsp cocoa or cacao powder
1–2 tbsp erythritol blend, xylitol or stevia drops to taste (optional)

- Preheat the oven to 160°C/gas mark 3. Spread the hazelnuts on a baking tray and roast for 8–10 minutes (the nuts will release their oils and this will make a smoother spread).

- Place the hazelnuts in a blender or processor. I use my Nutribullet. Blend until smooth.

- Melt the chocolate and coconut oil together in the microwave, 20 seconds at a time until melted, then add this to the blender along with the hazelnuts. Blend until smooth.

- If you want a sweeter spread, you can add a little sweetener – personally I don't think it needs it. If you add sweetener it will thicken the chocolate spread.

- Store in the fridge in sterilised jars. It will go hard when left in the fridge so remember to serve at room temperature.

9.6g fat, 1.4g net carbohydrates (0.8 sugar), 1.2g fibre, 1.8g protein per 15g serving

RASPBERRY CHIA JAM

My mum makes a wonderful raspberry jam, using less than half the sugar of conventional jams, which I loved. The sharpness of flavour was fantastic. I missed this, especially if I was making a Victoria sponge, so I had to find a sugar-free alternative. I don't add any sweetener to this as I don't think it needs it, but feel free to add xylitol, erythritol or stevia to taste. This takes minutes to make and will keep for 2–3 weeks if refrigerated and stored in a sterilised jar. You can also use strawberries or blueberries.

Makes 1 large jar (approx. 400–500g)

200g raspberries (frozen work brilliantly)
2–3 tbsp chia seeds

Seriously, these are the only ingredients. Obviously if you have a very sweet tooth you could add a few drops of stevia liquid or a couple of teaspoons of xylitol, but really it is delicious as it is.

- Place the raspberries in a saucepan and heat on a medium heat, slightly squishing the raspberries as they warm.
- Once the raspberries have started to release their juice and break down, add your chia seeds.
- Stir for 1–2 minutes and it will start to thicken as the chia seeds absorb the liquid.
- Pour into your sterilised jar and store in the fridge.

0.9g fat, 0.8g net carbohydrates, 1.9g fibre, 0.7g protein per 15g serving

LEMON CURD

I make this in the slow cooker as I find it works well. If you don't have a slow cooker, you can make this in the traditional way, in a bain-marie, which is much quicker.

Makes 2 jars

100g butter
100g xylitol or erythritol blend (add more if you prefer it sweeter)
zest and juice of 4 large lemons (removing any pips)
4 eggs, beaten

- Place the butter, sweetener, lemon zest and juice in your pudding basin. Place in the slow cooker and turn to low. Pour in boiling water until it comes halfway up the basin. Leave for 20 minutes.

- Remove from the slow cooker and leave to cool for 5 minutes. Keep the slow cooker on as you will be returning the basin shortly.

- Pour the beaten eggs into the lemon mixture, beating continuously.

- Take a square of foil, larger than the top of the basin. Place over the basin and seal well with string, making sure it is tight.

- Place back into the slow cooker, keeping the temperature low. Add more boiling water around the basin, ensuring the water comes halfway up the bowl.

- Cook for 2–3 hours, stirring a couple of times to avoid any lumps (if you forget to stir and it goes lumpy or curdles, whisk well with a balloon whisk).

- The curd should be thick enough to hold when poured from the back of a spoon, but not thick and lumpy.

- Pour into sterilised jars. Cover with a layer of baking parchment before sealing with the lid.
- Once opened, store in the fridge.

21g fat, 0.8g net carbohydrates, 0.9g fibre, 0.4g protein per 15g serving

FRESH TOMATO RELISH

This will last up to 2–3 days in the fridge. Makes a really good topping for meat, fish or burgers. Also adds a nice flavour to a salad, especially when topped with feta cheese.

Makes 2 jars (approx. 1kg)

750g tomatoes, diced
6 sun-dried tomatoes, diced
6 spring onions, finely chopped
½ red pepper, finely diced
2 cloves of garlic, crushed
1 chilli, finely chopped
small handful of fresh parsley
small handful of fresh chives
6 tbsp extra virgin olive oil
3–4 tbsp white wine vinegar
black pepper

- Place all the vegetables and herbs in a bowl and combine.
- Mix the oil and white wine vinegar together and season with black pepper.
- Pour this over the vegetables and herbs, combine well and place in the fridge until needed. (It can also be frozen.)

7.3g fat, 3.5g net carbohydrates, 1.4g fibre, 0.8g protein per 100g

SAUCES, PESTO AND CONDIMENTS

EASY MAYONNAISE

You can make this with a stick blender or food processor. I make a basic mayonnaise and add seasoning and other flavourings such as garlic or chilli after the base is made. This gives me the flexibility to make up several different flavours to store in small containers.

Makes 1 jar (approx 350g)

2 egg yolks
3–4 tsp freshly squeezed lemon juice
300–500ml olive oil
seasoning to taste

- Using your stick blender in a tall container, add the egg yolks and whisk, before adding the olive oil, drizzle by drizzle. You want to give the mixture time to whizz and thicken before adding more olive oil.
- Continue until you have the consistency you require.
- Add lemon juice and seasoning to taste.

85g fat, 0.1g net carbohydrates, 0g fibre, 1g protein per 100g

ALL-PURPOSE TOMATO SAUCE

This is a real gem and so easy to make. Perfect for using up overripe tomatoes or when you see tomatoes on offer in the supermarket. You can make this in a saucepan – if so use fresh herbs – but the slow cooker is so easy. Feel free to change the herbs to suit your own preference.

This can be used as a pasta sauce, the base for a bolognaise or lasagne, a topping for pizza or base for any other Italian-inspired dish.

Makes 2 jars (approx. 1kg)

1kg tomatoes, chopped
1 large red onion, chopped
2–3 cloves of garlic, roughly chopped
1 red pepper, diced
150ml red wine or stock
½ tsp dried thyme
½ tsp dried oregano
1 tsp dried parsley
1 tsp xylitol or erythritol
sprinkle of salt and pepper

- Preheat the slow cooker, referring to the manufacture's instructions.
- Add all the ingredients and combine well.
- Set the temperature to low and cook for 8–10 hours.
- When cooled, freeze or store in the fridge in an airtight container for up to 3–4 days.

0.1g fat, 3.6g net carbohydrates, 1g fibre, 0.6g protein per 100g

TOMATO KETCHUP

This recipe does take a while to cook, as you need to reduce it down, but it is worth it. It will keep stored in airtight, sterilised jars for up to 6 months. I store mine in the fridge.

Slow cooker – You can make this in the slow cooker, but you do need to sauté the vegetables first and omit the added water. Cook on low for 6–8 hours.

Makes 3 jars

1 tsp coconut oil or 1 tbsp olive oil
1 large red onion, diced
1 stick of celery, trimmed and diced
½ carrot, diced
2 cloves of garlic, sliced
½ fresh red chilli, deseeded and finely chopped (optional)
500g cherry tomatoes, diced
400g tin of chopped tomatoes
8 sun-dried tomatoes
1 tbsp tomato paste
1 tsp paprika
½ tsp onion powder
½ tsp garlic powder
½ tsp dried oregano
1 bay leaf
150ml apple cider vinegar
300ml water
70g Sukrin Gold
seasoning to taste

- Place the oil in a heavy based saucepan and heat gently on a medium heat. Add the onion, celery, carrot, garlic and chilli.

- Cook gently for 5 minutes before adding the tomatoes.

- Cook for another 5–10 minutes, or until the tomatoes start to break down and ooze their juices.

- Add all the remaining ingredients. Season to taste.

- Cook gently until the mixture has reduced by about half. This may take up to 45 minutes. Don't be tempted to increase the temperature above a medium heat as you don't want it to burn, you just want a very gentle simmer.

- Remove the bay leaf. Use a stick blender and whizz until smooth – you can use a liquidiser if you prefer. If you like a fine sauce, pop it through a sieve before placing back in the saucepan.

- If you find it is not thick enough, either give it a longer cook or you can add some cornflour (mix a tablespoon with some water to form a paste before adding to the mixture). Low carb/grain free can use coconut flour or xanthan gum.

- When it is at the correct thickness, taste and season again if needed. If you find it too acidic, add a little more sweetener or a few more sun-dried tomatoes.

- Store in sterilised jars.

0.3g fat, 0.7g net carbohydrates, 0.3g fibre, 0.2g protein per 15g serving

SUN-DRIED TOMATO & BASIL PESTO

If you love pesto but don't want the added cheese, this recipe is perfect. It delivers great flavour to wholemeal pasta, as a topping for a pizza or stuffed in a chicken breast.

Makes 1 small jar (approx. 200g)

125g sun-dried tomatoes
1 large handful of fresh basil
75g pine nuts
3–4 cloves of garlic
4 tbsp extra virgin olive oil (or the oil from the sun-dried tomatoes)
seasoning to taste

- Place all the ingredients in your food processor or blender and whizz until smooth and combined.

- Pour into a dish, cover, and place in the fridge for at least 30 minutes, allowing the flavours to infuse.

- Store in the fridge in an airtight container until ready to use. You can also freeze this. I normally place in a silicon ice-cube tray and pop out a few cubes when I need them.

28g fat, 2g net carbohydrates, 3.3g fibre, 2.7g protein per serving

SUN-DRIED TOMATO PASTE

Sun-dried tomato paste often contains unwanted sugar. However it is really simple to make yourself. You can store in a jar or even place into a silicon ice-cube mould, ready to pop out 'sun-dried tomato' cubes whenever you need to add some to your dish.

NB: I ask you to drain the sun-dried tomatoes from the oil in the jar because it is often vegetable or sunflower oil and it is far healthier to have olive oil in your food.

Makes 1 small jar

1 jar of sun-dried tomatoes (drained of oil, leaving approx. 150g)
2 cloves of garlic
1 tsp dried oregano
3 tbsp olive oil
seasoning to taste

- Simply whizz all the ingredients in a food processor until smooth.
- Store in a sterilsed jar or ice-cube mould.

3.2g fat, 3.1g net carbohydrates, 1.3g fibre, 0.7g protein per 15g serving

RED THAI PASTE

This is a nice paste that can add flavour to a lot of dishes. Add to chicken, soups or noodles. If you are giving this to children, you may want to adjust the chilli content.

Makes 1 small jar

4 tbsp olive oil
3 chillies, finely chopped
4 cloves of garlic
½ red onion, chopped
2cm piece of fresh ginger
3 stalks of lemongrass
juice and zest of 1 lime
3 tbsp paprika
3 tsp cumin seeds
3 tsp coriander seeds
3–4 sun-dried tomatoes
1 small bunch of fresh coriander

- Place all the ingredients in a food processor and whizz to form a paste.
- Place in a sterilised jar and store in the fridge for up to 2–3 weeks.

2.7g fat, 0.9g net carbohydrates, 0.5g fibre, 0.4g protein per 15g serving

SPICE BLENDS

It is a sad fact that many of the spice blends in our supermarkets contain added sugar. It is frustrating as we really don't need it and it's time the food manufacturers recognised this. In the meantime, do as I do and make up your own spice mixes. I store these in small jars until needed. All these recipes can be doubled or even tripled if you want to store in larger jars.

Place all the ingredients into a bowl and combine well before storing in your airtight jar.

CAJUN SPICE MIX

2 tsp garlic powder

3 tsp paprika

1 tsp onion powder

1 tsp cayenne pepper

2 tsp dried oregano

1 tsp chilli powder

½ tsp salt

½ tsp black pepper

CURRY POWDER

6 tsp ground coriander

3 tsp ground cumin

4 tsp turmeric

1 tsp ground mustard seeds

½ tsp ground ginger

1 tsp chilli powder (add more if you like it very hot)

½ tsp garlic powder

½ tsp onion powder

½ tsp ground nutmeg

½ tsp cayenne pepper

MOROCCAN SEASONING

3 tsp paprika

1 tsp ground cinnamon

½ tsp garlic powder

½ tsp onion powder

1 tsp ground cumin

2 tsp ground coriander

½ tsp cayenne pepper

½ tsp allspice

ITALIAN SEASONING

4 tsp dried oregano

2 tsp dried thyme

1 tsp dried basil

4 tsp dried parsley

1 tsp garlic powder

½ tsp onion powder

INDEX

THE
IMPR⟳VEMENT
ZONE

Looking for life inspiration?

The Improvement Zone has it all, from **expert advice** on how to advance your **career** and boost your **business**, to improving your **relationships**, revitalising your **health** and developing your **mind**.

Whatever your goals, head to our website now.

www.improvementzone.co.uk

INSPIRATION ON THE MOVE

INSPIRATION DIRECT TO YOUR INBOX